EVERYDAY COURAGE

50 Devotions to Build a Bold Faith

JOHN BEVERE

THOMAS NELSON
Since 1798

Published in Nashville, Tennessee, by Thomas Nelson. Thomas Nelson is a registered trademark of HarperCollins Christian Publishing, Inc.

Author is represented by the literary agency of The Fedd Agency, Inc., P. O. Box 341973, Austin, Texas 78734.

Thomas Nelson titles may be purchased in bulk for educational, business, fund-raising, or sales promotional use. For information, please email SpecialMarkets@ThomasNelson.com.

Unless otherwise noted, Scripture quotations are taken from the New King James Version®. Copyright © 1982 by Thomas Nelson. Used by permission. All rights reserved.

Scripture quotations marked AMPC are taken from the Amplified® Bible. Copyright © 1954, 1958, 1962, 1964, 1965, 1987 by The Lockman Foundation. Used by permission. www.Lockman.org.

Scripture quotations marked ESV are taken from the ESV® Bible (The Holy Bible, English Standard Version®). Copyright © 2001 by Crossway, a publishing ministry of Good News Publishers. Used by permission. All rights reserved.

Scripture quotations marked GNT are taken from the Good News Translation in Today's English Version—Second Edition. Copyright © 1992 by American Bible Society. Used by permission.

Scripture quotations marked MSG are taken from *THE MESSAGE*. Copyright © 1993, 2002, 2018 by Eugene H. Peterson. Used by permission of NavPress. All rights reserved. Represented by Tyndale House Publishers, a Division of Tyndale House Ministries.

Scripture quotations marked NIV are taken from the Holy Bible, New International Version®, NIV®. Copyright © 1973, 1978, 1984, 2011 by Biblica, Inc.® Used by permission of Zondervan. All rights reserved worldwide. www.zondervan.com. The "NIV" and "New International Version" are trademarks registered in the United States Patent and Trademark Office by Biblica, Inc.®

Scripture quotations marked NLT are taken from the Holy Bible, New Living Translation. Copyright © 1996, 2004, 2015 by Tyndale House Foundation. Used by permission of Tyndale House Ministries, Carol Stream, Illinois 60188. All rights reserved.

Any internet addresses, phone numbers, or company or product information printed in this book are offered as a resource and are not intended in any way to be or to imply an endorsement by Thomas Nelson, nor does Thomas Nelson vouch for the existence, content, or services of these sites, phone numbers, companies, or products beyond the life of this book.

ISBN 978-1-4002-4417-1 (audiobook)
ISBN 978-1-4002-4415-7 (eBook)
ISBN 978-1-4002-4416-4 (HC)

Printed in India

24 25 26 27 28 REP 10 9 8 7 6 5 4 3 2 1

―――――

Dedicated to our handsome and beautiful grandchildren:

Asher Alexander, Sophia Grace, Lizzy Hope, Augustus Michael, Scarlett Elizabeth, and Azariah Jacks

And to our grandson, who is now rejoicing in the presence of Jesus, and to the future ones to come!

May you always abide in God's love and holy fear

―――――

Contents

Contents

Contents

In the fear of the LORD there is strong confidence.

PROVERBS 14:26

Introduction

Let's talk about courage.

We live in a world where anxiety and anger run rampant. People are filled with stress and worry, and even churches have become fearful. Our cancel culture silences nonconformists while our Christian culture too often submits to the world's values. Every day there are men and women leaving the church or refusing to speak out with biblical truth.

As persecution increases in our nation, Christians will need courage now more than ever.

We are told those who stand in awe of God are "confident and fearless" (Psalm 112:8 NLT). For years our church fathers and mothers have affirmed that the fear of God swallows up all other fears, including the most destructive: the fear of man. The awe of God strengthens and emboldens our faith to stay true to Him. To state it simply, our courage rises according to our depth of godly fear. My hope is that this book inspires courage that won't fail, no matter the difficulty.

Thirty years ago, as a young man who battled and often succumbed to intimidation, I began a journey to discover what holy fear truly looked like. In the process my courage grew to the place that shocked not only myself, but my family and friends. The fear of the Lord was the secret, the fuel that propelled courage.

I discovered we will serve whom we fear. If we fear God, we will obey Him; if we fear man, we will ultimately obey men's desires. Through this journey I've learned how the virtue of fearing the Lord can transform your life into something wildly beautiful.

Before we begin, I want to clarify that the fear of the Lord does not mean we're scared of God. Our Creator desires a relationship of intimacy with every single one of us, and we cannot have intimacy with somebody we're afraid of. The person who's *scared of* God has something to hide; the person who *fears* God has nothing to hide. It's more like saying that person is afraid of being *away from* God.

I've explored this message in depth in my book *The Awe of God*, and now I want to share with you some of what I've learned about courage on my journey. I pray it will strengthen you for our current time and for what is coming. I truly believe we are living in the days where great heroes of the kingdom will manifest. I believe you are one of them!

The past heroes of the kingdom experienced great victories through their faith, but in their obedience to God, many were mocked, tortured, imprisoned, exiled, or rejected. Why? They lived in a fallen world that was hostile to the kingdom of God (Hebrews 11:36–39). But they all had this in common: out of their holy fear they refused to turn away from obedience, even if it meant suffering. They were confident in this promise: "Those who plant in tears will harvest with shouts of joy . . . they sing as they return with the harvest" (Psalm 126:5–6 NLT).

That is the same sort of confidence we need every day. We need courage to obey God's commands, to overcome discouragement, to be in His presence.

Jesus asked His disciples to follow Him. He invites you and me every day to do the same! So let's follow Him and discover the everyday courage He gives us.

PART 1

When You Need Courage in the Face of Fears

DAY 1

A Cure for Chaos

"Take courage! It is I. Don't be afraid."

MATTHEW 14:27 NIV

P icture this: it's the middle of the night, you and your companions are in the middle of a tumultuous sea, the wind is blowing with fury, and the waves are crashing against the boat. You're "in trouble" (Matthew 14:24 NLT), and all your companions know it. If that's not enough, suddenly everyone on board sees something eerie, something walking on the water. You don't know if it is a spirit or a person, but surely it can't be a person, for no one has ever done such a thing.

Terrified, you and your companions cry out in fear: "'It's a ghost!'" (v. 26 NIV). The mysterious figure on water responds with these words, "Take courage! It is I. Don't be afraid." Can you imagine hearing Jesus say these words to you in the midst of this terrifying moment?

This is not an example of the fear of God, but rather, the spirit of fear. The fear of the Lord, as you will learn, is something far different.

What do you think about when you hear the phrase "the fear of God"? Does it sound like Old Testament lingo that no longer relates to us? Or does it conjure images of people running away from an all-powerful, all-consuming holy God? Do you picture all the people pleading to get into Noah's ark when a torrential rain started falling, or the cities of Sodom and Gomorrah panicking while being destroyed for their wickedness?

While all these people surely lived in fear of God's judgment and wrath, the fear of the Lord isn't about being afraid of God. It's also not an archaic term reserved for the Old Testament.

The fear of the Lord is what protects our spirit and thoughts during days when the world seems to be in complete chaos. It's incredibly relevant to our lives right now, in this moment we're in.

Most people don't like hearing the word *fear*. But we must not confuse the spirit of fear with the fear of God. The Bible says we perfect holiness in the fear of the Lord and that we work out our salvation with fear and trembling (2 Corinthians 7:1; Philippians 2:12).

The fear the disciples had from seeing someone walking on water? That was the spirit of fear. But Mary Magdalene's desire to be with Jesus after the crucifixion, even in the face of danger? That was someone who feared God.

Even after witnessing the devastation of Jesus' death on the cross—the same Jesus who had delivered her from demonic possession—Mary remained faithful to Him. She longed to be with Him, even if it meant going to His body in the tomb to give it a proper burial. But upon arriving, she discovered an empty tomb and became distraught, believing someone had taken Jesus' body. A man at the tomb asked her, "Woman, why are you weeping?" (John 20:13).

At first Mary thought the man was a gardener. But then He spoke her name: "Mary" (v. 16).

There was Jesus, standing before her. Mary moved to embrace her Lord, not wanting to let Him go. She had so desperately desired to be in His presence, and she was rewarded for her devotion by becoming the first person to see the resurrected Savior.

Despite the chaos that resulted from Christ's death on the cross—a time when His followers could have so easily been afraid—Mary didn't run away from Jesus. Rather, she ran to Him. Her example is one we need to follow in the craziness of our current times. God gave Mary the courage to proclaim, "I have seen the Lord!" (v. 18 NIV). He will give you that courage too.

Dear heavenly Father, You long for us to long for You. May I run to You in the chaos of our times. Give me the strength to pursue Your will in my life, and fill me with Your Spirit. In Jesus Christ's name, amen.

Reject the Fear
of Rejection

**Fearing people is a dangerous trap, but
trusting the Lord means safety.**

PROVERBS 29:25 NLT

Early on in ministry while serving in my local church, I was terribly bound to *the fear of man*. I didn't realize how deeply enslaved I was until the Holy Spirit exposed my heart. Serving in a high-profile position in our megachurch, I connected with many individuals and was always quick to give a compliment, even if it wasn't true. I hated confrontation and avoided it like a plague. Hearing reports that I was one of the most loving men in the church brought happiness and satisfaction to me.

One day I heard the Lord say, *John, people say you are a loving and kind man.* But the way God spoke this to my heart didn't seem to be affirming.

"Yes, they do say that," I said with caution.

God responded, *Do you know why you speak nice and complimentary things to people even if they aren't true?*

"Why?"

Because you fear their rejection. So who is the focus of your love—you or them? If you really loved people, you would speak truth and not lie, even at the personal expense of being rejected.

I was stunned. Everyone else pegged me as a loving man, but the underlying truth was quite different. My motives were self-promoting, self-protecting, and self-rewarding. I was being a hypocrite in my behavior.

The fear of the Lord is a gift from God that keeps our motives and intentions in check. It protects us from hypocrisy because it alerts us to the thoughts, words, or actions stemming from the fear of man, which often leads to insincerity.

The story of Ananias and Sapphira in Acts 5 is an example of such a thing.

In the early days of the Christian church, believers shared their possessions to care for one another. They often sold land or houses and gave the profits to those in need. Ananias and his wife, Sapphira, were part of this group, and Scripture tells us they sold a piece of property but kept part of the money for themselves.

"This is far too much money to part with," they reasoned. "But we want to *appear* to give it all. So let's give only a portion, but say it's everything we received."

This couple didn't consider that God could see into their

The fear of the
Lord is a gift from
God that keeps
our motives and
intentions in
check.

hearts and minds, that the Lord would know what they were doing. And it cost them their lives—they were both buried the same day!

Ananias and Sapphira's actions weren't their downfall; their motivation was. They were *projecting* a certain image that was untrue in order to impress their community. It's something that's easy to do, even as believers.

Why do we say or do the things we do? What motivates us when we're around others? Remember that our only protection from any form of hypocrisy is the fear of God. We will not hide sin if we fear God more than the opinions of men.

Dear heavenly Father, forgive me for being more concerned with what others think than what You think. Help me to be focused on what You desire rather than my own temporary comfort. Let me esteem Your Word over man's words. In Jesus' name, amen.

Following Christ at All Costs

> The fear of the Lord is a fountain of life, to
> turn one away from the snares of death.
>
> PROVERBS 14:27

It's one thing to discover Jesus Christ and follow Him. It's quite another to keep following Him, even if that means certain death.

The disciple Andrew is a great example of this. Even though there's not a lot written about him, Andrew is noteworthy for being the first disciple to follow Jesus. Scripture tells us he found his brother Peter and announced, "We have found the Messiah" (John 1:41–42). Andrew was saying, "We have found the Anointed One"—the perfect Priest, the perfect Prophet, and the perfect King.

Just like most of the disciples, Andrew fled for his life the night Jesus was arrested. Yet this one act of cowardice wouldn't define him. After Jesus' resurrection, Andrew preached in

Ethiopia, which was under Roman rule and a great threat to Christ's disciples.[1] While preaching in Greece, he was told by the governor to stop. When he refused, he was sentenced to death by crucifixion. He requested to hang on an X-shaped cross since he felt unworthy to die on a cross similar to Jesus'.

History records Andrew as saying these words as he was being led to his death: "O cross, most welcomed and longed for! With a willing mind, joyfully and desirously, I come to you, being the scholar of Him which did hang on you, because I have always been your lover and yearned to embrace you."[2]

This wasn't the same man who ran for his life when Jesus was arrested. Andrew had changed. In fact, all the disciples who fled, except John, were eventually killed for their testimony of Jesus Christ. God granted them the privilege and courage to face the very things they ran from.

It's comforting to know that God can turn our failures into victories. As Philippians 1:6 states, "He who has begun a good work in you will complete it until the day of Jesus Christ." Even though we probably won't ever face something as terrifying as what Andrew had to endure, we still can be strengthened with the same courage that fueled him. When we seek God's will and ask for that strength, God will empower us by His grace to be bold through any circumstances we're dealing with.

Dear Father in heaven, please embolden me to walk in the strength You provide Your servants. Help me to be a witness for Your glory. Forgive me for the times when I have been fearful and worried about life's difficulties. Empower me to always follow You. In Jesus' name, amen.

DAY 4

Courage When It Counts

All these people died still believing what God had promised them. They did not receive what was promised, but they saw it all from a distance and welcomed it. . . . They were too good for this world.

HEBREWS 11:13, 38 NLT

In the African city of Carthage around the year AD 203, a Roman procurator (similar to a modern-day attorney) faced a young, imprisoned woman and demanded that she offer a sacrifice for the well-being of the emperors.

"I will not," she said with defiance.

Twenty-two-year-old Vibia Perpetua was a new mother and came from a prosperous family in Carthage. In a town where Christianity was forbidden, the procurator asked her a deadly question.

"Are you a Christian?"

"I am," Perpetua replied.

As her father begged her to recant her statement, the Roman authority ordered him to be beaten with a rod, then he passed sentence on Perpetua and her friends. As she wrote in her journals, "We were condemned to the beasts, and we returned to prison in high spirits."[1]

Can you imagine being this courageous? Even though Perpetua knew they were about to be brought to the Roman arena to be devoured by wild animals, she still remained in "high spirits." Up to the very end, she kept her faith.

Brought to the amphitheater, stripped and wearing only a net, Perpetua was first mauled by a wild bull, then stabbed by a gladiator yet she remained alive. She guided the novice gladiator's hand to her neck in order to finish the job. Perpetua didn't fear death; she embraced it.

Perpetua had the same bold faith as those found in the faith hall of fame in Hebrews 11—a list of familiar names like Abraham, Sarah, Isaac, Jacob, Joseph, and Moses. The people of Israel not only had faith when marching through the Red Sea to escape the Egyptians who were pursuing them; they also had faith when marching around Jericho for seven days until the walls came crashing down.

What sort of faith did it take for men like Gideon and Samson and David and Daniel to overthrow kingdoms and shut the mouths of lions and escape death by the sword? How could they be tortured yet refuse to turn from God in order to be set free? How did these men and women endure humiliation and beatings and imprisonment? Some ended up being stoned, others sawed in half, and others killed by the sword.

"[The saints] were looking for a better place, a heavenly homeland."

HEBREWS 11:16 NLT

What did these saints all have in common? None of them felt at home here on earth.

Hebrews 11:13–16 sums up the key to all their bravery:

All these people died still believing what God had promised them. They did not receive what was promised, but they saw it all from a distance and welcomed it. They agreed that they were foreigners and nomads here on earth. . . . They were looking for a better place, a heavenly homeland. (NLT)

Before she was sent to the arena, Perpetua wrote these words: "I realized that it was not with wild animals that I would fight but with the Devil, but I knew that I would win the victory."

She knew this earth wasn't her home; her home was before the throne of God. That's our home as well.

Dear gracious heavenly Father, I know You have something far better in mind for us other than this world. Thank You for the examples of the heroes of the faith who wandered over deserts and fled to mountains and hid in caves and holes for Your kingdom. Heroes who were too good for this world. Give me the courage You gave them. In Jesus' name, amen.

DAY 5

Fight Destructive Fears

Be strong in the grace that is in Christ Jesus.

2 TIMOTHY 2:1

What do you fear the most? Losing all your money and possessions, or losing a spouse or loved one? The fear of missing out (FOMO), or for the safety of your kids? These fears only lead to detrimental and unnecessary destruction.

The fear of God eradicates all other destructive fears. It also enhances our lives—both now and eternally. It illuminates the path to a good and fulfilling life.

If there's ever been a generation that's understandably fearful, it's this one. There is so much happening in the world that is unsettling, confusing, and anxiety-producing. And we now have the technology to know about all of it. But being fearful won't help you. It will actually paralyze you. I know because I've been there, afraid and anchored to the ground, unable to move.

I was once speaking in a new city, and after I had finished

with the service, I came back to my hotel room where thoughts began to bombard my mind. For some reason, I had an onslaught of dark thoughts about death.

I thought of a great minister I had just seen.

He's buried three of his children.

And then another God-fearing pastor came to mind.

His son was electrocuted and killed.

Then followed thoughts of a third godly leader I knew.

His son died in a car accident.

Even more tragedies involving ministers' children continued to fill my mind.

As I sat on the edge of the bed and removed one of my dress shoes, my body began to tremble. I thought of my own sons.

What if something like that happens to them? If it can happen to these great ministers, it can surely happen to me.

I was overwhelmed and paralyzed by this fear. And then the Holy Spirit spoke to me.

John, if there's an area you have fear in, you're still holding it, you still own it. You haven't put it at the foot of the cross.

It was true. I hadn't fully committed our sons to God, and therefore was subjected to destructive fears attacking my mind and consequently paralyzing me. Fears that weren't even a reality. I realized in that moment that I am not big enough to protect my boys—only God is.

I jumped up off the bed, one shoe still in hand, and screamed as loud as I could, "Addison, he's not mine! Austin, he's not mine!

Nor Alec; he's not mine!" (Arden was not born yet, but God knew I was speaking of any children we might have in the future.)

"God, they're all yours!" I shouted. "I'm just a steward over them. You may do whatever You want with them. I won't be possessive of them—even if You take them halfway around the world. Even if You take them to heaven. I will trust in You and not live in fear."

Then I paused before yelling again, "Devil—you're never killing them! You cannot touch them. They belong to Jesus!"

I've never feared for my sons' lives since. Never. Not once.

Take those destructive fears you have and place them at the foot of the cross. This is true humility, as we are told, "humble yourselves under the mighty hand of God . . . casting all your care upon Him, for He cares for you" (1 Peter 5:6–7).

Dear heavenly Father, help me be bold to pray and declare Your promises and Your will to be done. Please reveal anything in my life that I haven't yielded to You. Forgive me for the areas in my life that I still cling to in ownership that aren't under the lordship of Jesus. In Jesus' name, amen.

Freedom from Fear

Fear of the LORD leads to life, bringing
security and protection from harm.

PROVERBS 19.23 NLT

Imagine a life without a single worry or fear. Picture living each
moment in peace and confidence. Does this seem impossible
for you?

The potential we have in Jesus is full of unimaginable possi-
bilities. The fear of the Lord leads us to surrender all to God, and
in doing so we live a life so many others greatly desire. Not an
easy life without storms and sorrow, but one where we live above
our human potential.

Let's look at the example of Shadrach, Meshach, and
Abednego from the book of Daniel. Six hundred years before
Christ was born, Israel was ruled by King Nebuchadnezzar of
Babylon. He brought some of the finest Hebrew young men back
to Babylon to be trained in his court, and this included Shadrach,
Meshach, and Abednego.

King Nebuchadnezzar built a gold statue and commanded

everybody to fall on their knees to worship it when music was played. Anyone not kneeling and worshiping would immediately be thrown into a roaring furnace, he declared. Soon, word got back to the king that this trio of Israelites weren't complying with his dictate. He was informed, "These men are ignoring you, O king. They don't respect your gods and they won't worship the gold statue you set up" (Daniel 3:12 MSG).

King Nebuchadnezzar was furious, yet he gave them a second chance to obey and do what he had commanded. Did the three young men fear him? Not one bit.

They replied, "Your threat means nothing to us. If you throw us in the fire, the God we serve can rescue us from your roaring furnace and anything else you might cook up, O king. But even if he doesn't, it wouldn't make a bit of difference, O king. We still wouldn't serve your gods or worship the gold statue you set up" (vv. 16–18 MSG).

What amazing courage that produced astounding confidence! They remained calm and fearless even as they were hurled into the furnace. Later they walked out unharmed, without even the smell of smoke on them.

Though they faced death, they remained unafraid.

God is our Father, who delights in His children remaining brave in truth. Nothing pleases Him more than to see His children hold fast to confident hope and unshakable faith in adverse times. Imagine how pleased God was to see the courage of Shadrach, Meshach, and Abednego.

God is our Father, who delights in His children remaining brave in truth.

The apostle Paul had a similar attitude when he was faced with possible execution.

"I trust that my life will bring honor to Christ, whether I live or die. For to me, living means living for Christ, and dying is even better" (Philippians 1:20–21 NLT).

Remember that holy fear eradicates all other destructive fears, and it gives us the courage to delight in and obey the Lord and live up to the potential He has for us.

Dear heavenly Father, I can't imagine being put in a situation like the one Shadrach, Meshach, and Abednego were in. Please give me this strength of godly fear and courage to trust in You, not only in extreme cases, but in the challenges I will face today. Forgive me for the times I've feared others instead of fearing You. In Jesus' name, amen.

Chase Away All Other Fears

Make the Lord of Heaven's Armies holy in your life.
He is the one you should fear. He is the one who
should make you tremble. He will keep you safe.

ISAIAH 8:13–14 NLT

J ohn—you cannot preach."

The words from the pastor echoed in my head and made no sense. I had been invited to Monterrey, Mexico, to speak for a citywide evangelistic meeting. After I arrived to the venue early, a government official flanked by two uniformed officers told me I could only talk about tourist-related activities that night and nothing else. The pastor confirmed that the law said I couldn't preach without a permit if I wasn't a citizen. Normally, the law wasn't enforced, but for some reason the high-ranking official was enforcing it now.

"This can affect my church," the pastor said. "We better not let you preach."

I stepped outside to pray and plead to God for understanding.

"Father, I know You sent me down here. I need Your wisdom and counsel."

Then God quieted my mind enough to hear what I needed to do. When I went back into the building, the pastor confirmed that God had spoken to him and revealed that I needed to preach. When I stood before the large gathering, I didn't hesitate to proclaim the Word.

"Earlier I was ordered by an official to only talk to you about tourist-related activities," I said to the crowd. "So tonight I want to tell you about the greatest tourist to ever come to Mexico. His name is Jesus."

For the next hour, I preached about Jesus as Lord and Savior. Several people in the crowd responded to the call to receive Jesus Christ as Lord. The government official had sent two officers back to the auditorium to ensure I didn't preach and to apprehend me if I didn't comply, but when they saw the powerful things God was doing and the Word boldly proclaimed, the men who came to arrest me got saved!

If the pastor and I had given in to the threats from the government official, nobody would have been saved or ministered to that evening, including the officials sent to arrest me. God spoke to me through the Holy Spirit and gave me the courage to break through the intimidation wielded against me.

You most likely aren't going to be put in a situation today where you might be arrested for preaching the gospel. But you should keep this truth before you at all times: you will serve who you fear. If you fear God, you'll obey God. If you fear man, you'll ultimately obey man's desires.

The fear of God opens up the path to a life beyond anything you have ever imagined. And it's only when you have this holy fear that you are able to boldly address anything that life throws at you. In the words of Charles Spurgeon, "The fear of God is the death of every other fear; like a mighty lion, it chases all other fears before it."[1]

Dear heavenly Father, instill in me the boldness to not fear others but instead to fear You. May I always remember what Proverbs 29:25 says: "Fearing people is a dangerous trap" (NLT). Holy Spirit, please sear these words on my heart. In Jesus' name, amen.

DAY 8

Follow His Command

"You are My friends if you do whatever I command you."

JOHN 15:14

Hudson Taylor was thirty-three years old when he wandered out on the sands of a beach, burdened by spiritual agony, and finally agreed to God's calling on his life.

> I told Him (God) that all the responsibility as to issues and consequences must rest with Him; that as His servant, it was mine to obey and to follow Him—His to direct, to care for, and to guide me and those who might labor with me. Need I say that peace at once flowed into my burdened heart?[1]

This burden led Hudson Taylor to China, where he founded China Inland Mission and spent over five decades in ministry. His work helped create 125 schools and bring over 800 missionaries to the country.[2] But it wasn't without its hardships. Taylor endured many terrible losses—illnesses, persecution, even the death of his wife and several of his children. Yet he understood what his calling to God meant when he wrote, "Unless there is an element of risk in our exploits for God, there is no need for faith."[3]

Faith doesn't just come by putting our trust in God. It comes by following His commands. Did you know there are over five hundred commands in the New Testament alone? Though these aren't commands that are necessary for salvation—which is a free gift from God—when we follow these commands, we glorify God

Hudson Taylor took seriously the final words of Jesus, as recorded in Matthew 28:19–20: "Go therefore and make disciples of all the nations . . . teaching them to observe all things that I have commanded you." Taylor would say that the Great Commission was not an option up for consideration but rather a command to be obeyed.

Consider what it looks like to obey God's commands in your life. Are there divine instructions from God that could have a dramatic impact on your life, or others' lives, for God's glory?

Dear gracious Father, thank You for the lives of heroic leaders of the faith. Show me what You want for my life, and help me follow Your commands. Forgive me for not obeying or even knowing the commands You have for me. In Jesus' name, amen.

Pursue God's Word

Above all, you must realize that no prophecy
in Scripture ever came from the prophet's
own understanding, or from human initiative.
No, those prophets were moved by the
Holy Spirit, and they spoke from God.

2 PETER 1:20–21 NLT

Courage comes from the Word of God, and nothing will strengthen our hearts and spirits more than reading examples of the God-fearing faith found in the Bible. One such incredible story of courageous faith comes shortly before the very familiar and beloved story of David and Goliath.

Before young David even stepped on the field to face the Philistine giant Goliath, the king's son Jonathan and his armor-bearer demonstrated great courage when they attacked an entire garrison of Philistine soldiers.

The Israelites were at war with the mighty Philistine army, and they were vastly outnumbered. While "the Philistines mustered a massive army of 3,000 chariots, 6,000 charioteers, and as many warriors as the grains of sand on the seashore!" (1 Samuel 13:5 NLT), "none of the people of Israel had a sword or spear, except for Saul and Jonathan" (v. 22 NLT). So King Saul and the Israelites waited in fear, trying to determine their next move.

Jonathan, however, knew exactly what he needed to do. In 1 Samuel 14, he told his armor-bearer that they should make the dangerous trek over to the enemy garrison. "Maybe GOD will work for us. There's no rule that says GOD can only deliver by using a big army. No one can stop GOD from saving when he sets his mind to it" (v. 6 MSG).

Jonathan's armor-bearer shared his same faith. "Go ahead. Do what you think best. I'm with you all the way" (v. 7 MSG). What a fearless faith demonstrated by not only Jonathan but the man bearing his armor!

After a treacherous climb to the Philistine camp, the two men struck down around twenty of their enemies and created a panic among the pagans. When the Israelites heard the Philistines were running for their lives, they joined the chase, knowing God had saved them.

These two men had undaunted faith in God's complete power, and their example should invigorate us. Scripture is full of such bolstering examples, which is why we need to spend quality time reading and meditating on Scripture.

Let's marvel for a moment on the extraordinary Word of God. The sixty-six books of the Bible were written over a 1,500-year time span. God used over forty writers over that span of

Spending focused time in the Word of God, asking the Holy Spirit to teach us, is what gives us faith each and every day.

time from three different continents and writing in three different languages—enlisting kings, prisoners, soldiers, shepherds, farmers, and physicians. He even used a tax collector! Their words were compiled across time and distance to form a perfectly harmonized book.[1]

Only God could do something so miraculous. And we have that living, breathing miracle available at our fingertips at any time!

Spending focused time in the Word of God, asking the Holy Spirit to teach us, is what gives us faith each and every day. Faith comes by hearing God's Word, so open up your heart and make space for it. King David called the Word a light unto his path, a lamp to his feet (Psalm 119:105). It can be a light for your path too.

Dear heavenly Father, speak to me through Your holy Word, and fill me with the same courage that Jonathan and his armor-bearer had. I am told in the book of Romans that faith comes by hearing Your Word, so as I remain in the Scripture on a daily basis, enlarge my faith. Help me also never to forget that reading Your Word under the inspiration of the Holy Spirit will open my heart to know You intimately. I ask this in Jesus' name, amen.

Stay Armed and Ready

All Scripture is God-breathed and is useful for teaching, rebuking, correcting and training in righteousness, so that the servant of God may be thoroughly equipped for every good work.

2 TIMOTHY 3:16–17 NIV

Paul the apostle birthed and oversaw the growth of the massive church in Ephesus, Greece. He stood before his appointed leaders for what he knew would be his final meeting until heaven. They didn't have phones, texting, or emails, so the words he would leave them with would be crucial to their future growth.

His emphasis was for them to guard not only themselves but those they led. But from what? False leaders and believers who would come into their midst. People who would profess Christianity but cleverly pervert the purity of God's message of life. He warned them of this danger for three years and finally, the full responsibility of guarding the flock would be left to them. What was his final instruction? "So now, brethren, I commend you to God *and to the word of His grace*, which is able to build you up and give you an inheritance" (Acts 20:32, emphasis added).

Paul didn't just commend them to God, but also to the "word of His grace." Today the greatest protection from the dangers in this life are right there at your fingertips, ready to guide you in every aspect of your life. It's the perfect instruction manual for living. Yet too often we fail to open its pages and seek its wisdom.

Every day, we face a fresh battleground where we are tested. Second Timothy 3:1–5 in *The Message* gives us a good description of what we're up against:

> Don't be naive. There are difficult times ahead. As the end approaches, people are going to be self-absorbed, money-hungry, self-promoting, stuck-up, profane, contemptuous of parents, crude, coarse, dog-eat-dog, unbending, slanderers, impulsively wild, savage, cynical, treacherous, ruthless, bloated windbags, addicted to lust, and allergic to God. *They'll make a show of religion*, but behind the scenes they're animals. Stay clear of these people. (emphasis added)

These impostors will profess belief in Jesus but will live no different from the lost world. This aptly describes much of our Western faith culture today. Social media is full of the self-absorbed and self-promoting, yet they profess allegiance to Christ Jesus. Much of the business world is comprised of the dog-eat-dog and money-hungry mindsets, while many serve in their churches on weekends. A number of Christian men and a solid percentage of Christian women watch pornography on a regular basis.

In 1 Peter 4:1–2 (NKJV), Peter instructed us to arm ourselves for suffering. Can you imagine a military going to war without any planes, ships, tanks, guns, bullets, knives—unarmed? Just the thought of it seems ludicrous. It's just as crazy for a believer to be unprepared for the battleground of faith, yet many are.

Most of the early church's opposition came from those who professed to know God. Well, it's no different today. An unarmed believer will likely bypass hardship for the sake of self-preservation, which includes the desire to be accepted. The fear of the Lord is what arms us; it maintains a deep resolve in our will to obey God no matter what suffering it may entail.

So how do we arm ourselves? Paul tells us at the end of 2 Timothy 3: "All Scripture is God-breathed and is useful . . . so that the servant of God may be thoroughly equipped for every good work" (vv. 16–17 NIV). Yet it's not our knowledge of Scripture that's the key. There are people in the church who can quote verses and chapters of the Bible, yet when they meet difficult situations, they seek to protect themselves in their own way. They are captive to the fear of man.

It's not enough to only read Scripture; we must embrace it as our primary priority and obey it.

Dear heavenly Father, forgive me for not equipping myself the way I should. Help me to not just hear Your Word but to obey it. Strengthen me for what I might face in the world today. Thank You for Your love and protection. In Jesus' name, amen.

PART 2

When You Need Courage to Overcome

DAY 11

Fight Discouragement

How joyful are those who fear the L<small>ORD</small> and delight in obeying his commands. . . . They do not fear bad news; they confidently trust the L<small>ORD</small> to care for them. They are confident and fearless and can face their foes triumphantly.

PSALM 112:1, 7–8 NLT

Today is the day you're going to obliterate discouragement from your life.

One of the biggest battles we face is discouragement. Everybody has to fight this.

One day as I was praying, the Lord asked me to state aloud the opposite of courage.

"Fear, of course," I said.

No, it's discouragement, God whispered.

Suddenly, I saw the word *discourage* in a whole new light! We should view discouragement as the opposite of courage, and, therefore, it is to be given no place in our minds. Yet it's something we often tolerate. We don't recognize it as an enemy to our faith, so we pamper it and coddle it, we lean into it and feel sorry for ourselves when it comes.

But why? When we know that God is our source of joy and courage, we have no reason to fear or be discouraged. When discouragement inevitably comes knocking at our door, here's what we need to do: be strong and of good courage.

Think of a clear example of bravery in the Bible. Joshua was one of the children of Israel who left Egypt to embark on the great exodus. He and Caleb were among the twelve men sent from the tribes of Israel to spy out the land of Canaan. This was the land God promised to them. Yet ten of those spies didn't believe the Israelites could secure it. Only Joshua and Caleb declared with confidence that the Lord would surely deliver Canaan into their hands. All twelve leaders saw the same things, but they didn't see them the same way. Ten chose the path of their own ability, which led to discouragement, and only two saw God's ability.

This was the reason God said, "Be strong and of good courage" (Deuteronomy 3:16) to Joshua seven different times—whether it was through Moses, the elders, or God Himself—before entering the promised land. The Lord knew this would be one of Joshua's greatest challenges.

Discouragement occurs during the droughts in our lives. It arrives in the middle of the battle when we feel deserted by God.

The true enemies to the Israelites weren't the intimidating giants living in the promised land. No—the enemies were the insulting whispers in their minds to remain in fear.

Joshua and Caleb feared God more than any threatening enemy. Because of that, they became the only two original members of the exodus to enter and possess the promised land.

Dear heavenly Father, give me the courage to dispel discouragement with words of faith and hope from You. May I delight in the fear of You, for it is "a fountain of life, to turn one away from the snares of death" (Proverbs 14:27). In Jesus' name, amen.

Proclaim the Truth

Who are those who fear the LORD? He will
show them the path they should choose.

PSALM 25:12 NLT

I t takes courage to speak out. To not worry what others think
of you but rather to communicate in a way that honors God.
The story of John the Baptist and Herod offers an inspiring and
dramatic illustration of this.

John the Baptist was on a singular mission his entire life:
to point others to Jesus Christ. But it was one thing to proclaim
his Lord and Savior to a crowd gathered to hear him, and quite
another to stand up to Herod Antipas, the ruler of Galilee in
the Roman Empire. John didn't hesitate in rebuking Herod for
divorcing his wife and taking his brother's wife, Herodias, as his
own wife. John's public condemnation landed him in prison.

King Herod didn't want John the Baptist executed. He found
him fascinating, and he knew John had a lot of followers, which
might lead to rebellion if he killed the prophet. However, at a
party, a drunken Herod vowed to give the daughter of Herodias

anything she wanted. The girl sought her mother's advice and asked for John's head on a platter.

John knew the consequences of speaking against Herod, yet he never hesitated to tell the truth in public. The king, however, feared what the people around him might think. Although Herod didn't want to kill John the Baptist—the request even saddened him—he agreed to have John executed in the dark depths of the prison to save face with the people.

A. T. Robertson, a preacher and Bible scholar, said this about John speaking out against Herod: "It cost him his head, but it is better to have a head like John's and lose it than to have an ordinary head and keep it."[1]

We might not have to worry about risking our physical lives, but speaking biblical truth can cause us real hardships— emotional, financial social, or otherwise. Don't hesitate to be strong and authentic. Be open and honest about the truth you know, and proclaim it when you can. God will give you courage to speak up and proclaim truth.

Dear heavenly Father, keep me strong today with my thoughts and actions. Help me to know the right words to speak to others, and guide me with how I can be a witness for Jesus. Keep my heart strong in a world full of hate and lies. In Jesus' name, amen.

Be Ready for the Storms

In the fear of the LORD there is strong confidence,
and His children will have a place of refuge.

PROVERBS 14:26

It is very easy to let the troubles of today consume our hearts and minds. We hear news reports of the strife and hatred in our world. We have friends going through hardships. Our work brings up daily issues. And we often struggle to keep our families together.

In the midst of everyday madness, Jesus gives us a command: "Peace, be still" (Mark 4:39).

Three words. That's all it took for Jesus to silence the storms threatening Him and the disciples in their boat on the sea. The disciples went from shaking at the threat of the storm to shaking at the power this Man had just displayed. Even the wind and waves obeyed Jesus.

During our turbulent times, or when we feel anxious or overwhelmed, remember, just as Jesus spoke to the storm, He's given you the power to speak to the storm raging against you in His name!

But Jesus didn't just simply say those comforting words and end it there. He also rebuked His disciples: "Why are you afraid? Do you still have no faith?" (Mark 4:40 NLT).

God knew the storm would arise because He knows the end from the beginning. He had directed Jesus and the disciples into the boat with the full knowledge of the danger that awaited them. Yet God also gave the disciples the authority and power to rule over the storm—and they responded in fear.

When the fierce wind and waves crashed around them, they could have stood at the bow of the boat without fear and shouted at the top of their lungs, "Storm, you are not going to harm us, nor will you stop us! We're making it to the other side because Jesus said we're going to the other side. So get out of our way!"

The downpours and disturbances in our lives can come out of nowhere. Perhaps it's your health, finances, marriage, children, job, school, rejection, or persecution for your faith.

Remember this: God never leads us into a storm that He doesn't give us the power to overcome. Struggles and turmoil and conflicts are inevitable, but what separates those who are defeated in life from those who triumph is the knowledge that we can face with boldness whatever may come against us.

When you're feeling anxious or overwhelmed, don't forget that our King is the One who calms the storm, but He waits for us to speak His word in faith!

God never leads us into a storm that He doesn't give us the power to overcome.

Dear Lord, forgive me for forgetting that You have given me authority, in Your name, to speak to the adversities of life. You have given me the power to rule over the storms that would attack my life and purpose. I choose to trust You and walk away from any fears and anxieties today. In Jesus' name, amen.

Be Strong and Courageous

Be strong and courageous. Do not be afraid or terrified because of them, for the Lᴏʀᴅ your God goes with you; he will never leave you nor forsake you.

DEUTERONOMY 31:6 ɴɪᴠ

Do you ever feel like godly courage, the kind you read about in Scripture and hear about in sermons, is only for heroes and heroines of the faith? Do you ever sense that courage in Christ can only come after years of walking with Him and maturing as a believer?

The truth is courage is for any believer at any time in their faith. Courageous faith born out of the holy fear of God will empower you when you need it most. Rahab is a beautiful example of this. Her story in Joshua 2 has all the makings of an epic movie like *Gladiator*.

The Israelites were preparing to move into the promised land of Canaan, and blocking their way was the walled, pagan city of Jericho. The leader of the Israelites after Moses' death, Joshua,

Courage
is for any
believer at
any time in
their faith.

sent two young men to spy out the city, and they ended up hiding out at the house of a prostitute named Rahab. When the king of Jericho was told there were spies at this prostitute's house, he ordered them to come out. In a bold move, fearing God instead of man, Rahab lied and told the king that the spies had already left—and he should hurry to leave and catch them.

When the king's men left, and the spies were safe, Rahab revealed her reason for protecting them: "I know that the LORD has given you the land" (Joshua 2:9).

She didn't say, "I know you *said* that God gave you this land," Nor did she say, "*If* God has really given you this land." Rather, she truly believed that God was going to give the land to the Israelites because of everything God had already done for them. She put her life, and her family's life, on the line because she believed in the true God.

Rahab's story, of course, didn't end there. She eventually married Salmon from the tribe of Judah, and they had a son named Boaz. Ultimately, Rahab became the mother-in-law of Ruth and is part of the lineage of Jesus. Hebrews 11 includes her in the extraordinary list of the heroes of the faith, placing her among people like Moses, David, and Samuel.

Courageous faith can come to anybody when it comes out of the holy fear of our awesome God. The Lord emboldened Rahab to be strong in the midst of a great trial, and He never left her side. Be strong and courageous today, whatever you face, knowing that God is for you and with you.

Dear heavenly Father, thank You for giving courage to both the strong and the weak. Help me to always remember to have the wholehearted faith in You that Rahab demonstrated. Forgive me for any times I have questioned or doubted Your power. In Christ's name, amen.

The Strength to Resist

> God is greatly to be feared in the assembly of the saints, and to be held in reverence by all those around Him.

PSALM 89:7

World War II produced many heroes that history will always remember. Soldiers who died valiantly on fields of battle far from their homes. But like the heroes of the faith mentioned in Hebrews 11, there were brave men and women who took a stand against the evils of the day. Dietrich Bonhoeffer was one of those heroes.

As a German pastor and theologian, Bonhoeffer witnessed Adolf Hitler's rise to power in his country. Many German leaders in the church and the nation welcomed the rise of the Nazi party. However, Bonhoeffer opposed the Nazi ideology and spoke out against it. After becoming involved with the German resistance movement, he was arrested and executed in a concentration camp in April 1945.[1]

While spending time in German prisons before he was executed at the age of thirty-nine, Bonhoeffer wrote the following:

> I believe that God can and will bring good out of evil, even out of the greatest evil. For that purpose he needs men who make the best use of everything. I believe that God will give us all the strength we need to help us to resist in all the times of distress. But he never gives it in advance, lest we should rely on ourselves and not on him alone. A faith such as this should allay all our fears for the future.[2]

Watching Bonhoeffer's execution, the camp doctor described the final moments of this Christian martyr's life:

> I saw Pastor Bonhoeffer . . . kneeling on the floor praying fervently to God. I was most deeply moved by the way this lovable man prayed, so devout and so certain that God heard his prayer. At the place of execution, he again said a short prayer and then climbed the few steps to the gallows, brave and composed. His death ensued after a few seconds. In the almost fifty years that I worked as a doctor, I have hardly ever seen a man die so entirely submissive to the will of God.[3]

Dietrich Bonhoeffer's impact on Christianity since his death has been profound. He left behind a legacy of courage and faith in all his writings, such as his classic *The Cost of Discipleship.*

Men and women like Bonhoeffer are examples for us to follow. Even if our country isn't involved in a physical war, we are always in a spiritual war, with battles being fought every moment of the day. But remember, as Bonhoeffer said, God gives us the strength to resist evil.

Who are some heroes of faith that inspire you? How can you be strong and victorious today in your spiritual battles?

Dear heavenly Father, I praise You for being in control of my life. Help me to stand against the evils of this day and allay all destructive fears. Fill me with the strength to win the battles that I have today. In Jesus' name, amen.

Stand on a Firm Foundation

"On this rock [of knowledge revealed by God] I will build My church, and the gates of [hell] shall not prevail against it."

MATTHEW 16:18

I saw you with Jesus the Galilean."

In the middle of the courtyard by the crackling fire, the servant girl's words seared Peter's soul. With a crowd of faces staring at him, the disciple shook his head.

"I have no idea what you're talking about."

Later, as he slipped out toward the gate, another woman claimed the same thing: "This man was with Jesus."

"I don't know Him!" Peter shouted back. "I swear I've never seen Him before."

Not long after that, another stranger approached him. "You have to be one of them. I can tell by your accent—it gives you away."

Peter began to curse, his denial vehement and unwavering.

"I have no idea what you're talking about!"

Just then, as the rooster crowed, Peter remembered what Jesus had told him: "Before the rooster crows, you will deny Me three times" (Matthew 26:34).

Just like that, the great and mighty Peter crumbled. Weeping with guilt, he wandered off, his self-confidence gone. The declaration he had once made to Jesus surely echoed in his mind.

"Lord, I am ready to go with You, both to prison and to death" (Luke 22:33).

The story in Matthew 26 could have ended there. Yet Jesus had more plans for Peter. He had prayed that Simon Peter's faith would not fail after this spectacular act of public rejection. Jesus knew that out of this trial a new Peter would emerge, one who needed to fulfill his destiny and strengthen his brothers and sisters in Christ.

Being humbled and broken are necessary ingredients for receiving grace from God. It wouldn't be long before the angel of the Lord would speak to Mary Magdalene at the tomb and single Peter out: "But go, tell His disciples—and Peter—that He is going before you into Galilee; there you will see Him, as He said to you" (Mark 16:7).

After his repeated denials, Peter was shaken to the core, but the foundation that God had laid underneath remained. It was the sure foundation of Peter's understanding that Jesus was the Son of God—a foundation so sure that Peter later glorified God in his death.

How sturdy are your convictions, and how assured are your beliefs? Are they God-centered or founded in your own will-power? Although we may feel confident in our faith, there are people and circumstances that can shake us to our core just like they did Peter.

Our sure foundation is revealed in the Word of God, and it will be your rock for those times when you are tested and broken and shaken.

Dear heavenly Father, forgive my rejection and denial of You, both in public and in private. I am sorry for the times I have shrunk back or run away from adversity. In the heat of battle, I have lost sight of Jesus, and I'm so deeply sorry for this. Help me to stand on a firm foundation, one that cannot be shaken. In Jesus' name, amen.

Being humbled and broken are necessary ingredients for receiving grace from God.

DAY 17

Beware of Pride

[These people] through faith subdued kingdoms, worked righteousness, obtained promises, stopped the mouths of lions, quenched the violence of fire, escaped the edge of the sword, *out of weakness were made strong*.

HEBREWS 11:33–34 (EMPHASIS ADDED)

Some of the greatest and most courageous lessons in faith come after failure. Godly courage often arises in those who have previously shown great cowardice. The apostle Peter is one such example.

Peter had his shining moments. After all, he was the disciple who proclaimed of Jesus: "You are the Christ, the Son of the living God" (Matthew 16:16). He was also the one who, after toiling at sea all night with nothing to show for it, heeded Jesus' instruction to launch back out into deeper waters and cast his nets once again. Simon Peter was very hungry for the things of God and boldly asked questions when others stayed silent. He was the one who walked on water.

And Peter was also the one to deny Jesus. It's hard to believe, isn't it?

When Jesus told the disciples that "here at this table, sitting among us as a friend, is the man who will betray me" (Luke 22:21 NLT). How did the others respond? They discussed who it could be and that question led to an argument of who among them was the greatest. Can you believe that? Jesus had *just* told them He was about to be handed over to the chief priests to be condemned to death and delivered to the Romans to be mocked, scourged, and killed, and yet His closest friends were arguing like children

It's easy to guess who started this debate: Simon Peter. As A. W. Tozer wrote, "The man Peter had a reputation for being first because he was a most impetuous man. He was either the first or among the very first in almost everything that took place and that touched him while he was alive."[1] Peter was surely confident that he was the greatest of the twelve. This confidence, however, wasn't rooted in love; it was anchored in pride.

When we fear God, there is no room for pride. In fact, holy fear leads to true humility.

Peter had the courage to stand in front of the Roman army and cut off a soldier's ear. Yet when a little servant girl questioned him about Jesus, Peter denied Christ. It's easy to be courageous when everything is going the way you think it's supposed to go. It's much harder when your back is against the wall, things aren't going as planned, your sight is limited, and your reputation is at stake.

Fortunately, Peter's story wasn't over. After his denial of Christ and the pivotal moment when Jesus convicted him with a look (Luke 22:61), the apostle humbled himself, repented of his pride, and lived his faith boldly with an even more loyal heart.

Beware of pride and pursue humility, especially when your faith is challenged and there is much to overcome. When you are humble, it allows you to rely on God and trust in His grace to pull you through rather than on your own ability. To be clothed in humility is to wear His armor rather than your own. It will produce a strong boldness in you that will cause the enemy to tremble and run.

Dear heavenly Father, teach me to not only fear You but to be humble before You. Help me see how true, genuine humility makes me courageous. Thank You for examples of those who failed yet were forgiven and given grace, the same way You've forgiven me and given me grace. In Jesus' name, amen.

Be Transformed

You have been set free from sin.

ROMANS 6:18 NIV

When we are first introduced to Mary Magdalene in Luke 8, we see that she was traveling with Jesus and the twelve apostles from village to village spreading the good news. The only part of her past the Bible mentions is that Jesus cast out seven demons from her. No former offenses are listed; no grisly details are written down. We simply know that Christ liberated her from the bondage of sin.

This was the good news that Jesus and His band of followers were proclaiming: that repentance can produce restoration. Mary Magdalene was a living and breathing example of that. She exemplified Romans 6:18 (MSG): "All your lives you've let sin tell you what to do. But thank God you've started listening to a new master, one whose commands set you free to live openly in his freedom!"

One of the most beautiful and empowering words in the Bible is *repentance*. It speaks of promise and hope. It signals a new beginning. It's the starting point to receiving Jesus' free gift of grace that transforms our lives.

The danger is in standing on the starting line but never running the race. I personally believe one of the biggest obstacles we've created to enjoying a deep, intimate relationship with God is our formulated "sinner's prayer." Many people think, *I've prayed the sinner's prayer. I'm covered by the grace of God. I'll just try the best I can because Christians are really no different than sinners—we're just forgiven.*

This is so far from the truth Scripture reveals. We have been given the "divine nature" (2 Peter 1:4); it is our responsibility to walk in it. We are told to "lead a life worthy of [our] calling" (Ephesians 4:1 NLT). True holiness is a cooperation between deity and humanity. God supplies the grace, but we must cooperate, because grace empowers us to cleanse ourselves (2 Corinthians 7:1).

Grace—what a gift. Grace saves us. It grants us a new nature. It empowers us to live like Jesus. And it's something we can never earn. But it requires repentance, because without that we can't experience the life God has for us. Without repentance, we won't permanently walk away from a self-seeking lifestyle.

Here is the good news: when we humbly confess our sins and repent, God will forgive us and empower us to walk away from what once held us in bondage. We can overcome our past and the sins that keep us from being transformed.

Repentance isn't a sinner's prayer; it's a steady practice. With regular confession and the Holy Spirit's help, we can abandon our own ways and live according to Jesus.

Dear heavenly Father, it's only by the power of Your grace that I can live the godly life You have for me. Forgive me for trying to live this life on my own abilities. Give me the strength to set my life apart so it glorifies You. In Jesus' name, amen.

DAY 19

Strength for Hard Times

"It is the same with my word. I send it out, and it always produces fruit. It will accomplish all I want it to, and it will prosper everywhere I send it."

ISAIAH 55:11 NLT

In 1863, our nation was broken and bloodied, and President Abraham Lincoln found himself dejected and troubled. For two years the Civil War had decimated the country. Thousands of soldiers had died on the battlefield. Even though the Confederacy was outnumbered and unprepared for battling the Union, the excellent leadership of the Southern generals and the strong morale of the soldiers propelled the South to multiple victories.

After a visit to the War Department, Lincoln returned home with a heavy spirit. His wife noticed his distress.

"Did you hear any news?" Mary Todd Lincoln asked her husband.

"Yes, plenty of news, but no good news. It is dark, dark everywhere."

A year earlier, Lincoln's beloved eleven-year-old son, Willie, had passed away. The president still carried a profound grief inside of him.

On this occasion, Lincoln picked up a Bible and began to read it. After fifteen minutes, everything in his demeanor changed. Lincoln's face seemed more cheerful. Elizabeth Keckley, the seamstress to Mary Lincoln, recounted the scene in her memoir:

> The dejected look was gone, and the countenance was lighted up with new resolution and hope. The change was so marked that I could not but wonder at it, and wonder led to the desire to know what book of the Bible afforded so much comfort to the reader.[1]

Elizabeth discovered that Lincoln had been reading from the book of Job.

"What a sublime picture was this! A ruler of a mighty nation going to the pages of the Bible with simple Christian earnestness for comfort and courage, and finding both in the darkest hours of a nation's calamity."[2]

Abraham Lincoln knew the power found in the Scriptures. During his darkest moments, Lincoln found confidence in the Bible. "In regard to this Great Book," Lincoln said, "I have but to say, it is the best gift God has given to man. All the good the Savior gave to the world was communicated through this book."[3]

Believe in the power of Scripture to transform you and in the process change your outlook.

We all experience tough and difficult times in our lives. Where do you go when you feel despair or when your heart hurts? Do you attempt to console yourself with temporary, fleshly comforts or merely positive thinking, or do you believe in the power of Scripture to transform you and in the process change your outlook? Spend time in the Word today and believe, as Lincoln did, that it is the source of needed strength.

Dear heavenly Father, thank You for speaking to us through the Bible. I marvel at the fact that Your Word is holy and perfect. Forgive me for not going to Scripture during times when I'm overwhelmed and tired. Give me strength today for everything I will face. I ask this in Your Son's name, amen.

DAY 20

Overcome Defeat

Don't be intimidated in any way by your enemies. . . . For you have been given not only the privilege of trusting in Christ but also the privilege of suffering for him.

PHILIPPIANS 1:28–29 NLT

Imagine working in secret to get the Word of God out to the people, risking your very life to deliver the Scriptures to the public!

It may be hard for us in the free world today to imagine this reality and the accompanying risks when we have the Bible so easily available to us everywhere, including on our phones. We can access the Bible in almost any language at any time. But centuries ago, when the Bible was guarded by a few and not accessible to the average person, a courageous man risked numerous obstacles and defeat to get the Word to the masses.

William Tyndale was a scholar and a priest who became inspired to translate the Bible into English. In the sixteenth century, it was forbidden by law for the Bible to be translated into any language other than Hebrew and Greek. But on the heels of the

Reformation, which took place in the early 1500s and sparked a movement to make church doctrine and the Scriptures accessible to everyone, Tyndale was emboldened to overcome the barriers.

At first, he approached a bishop named Cuthbert Tunstall to help with the English translation, but the bishop rejected his request. So William Tyndale moved to Germany in 1524 to begin work on translating and printing the New Testament in English.

For the rest of his life, Tyndale encountered obstacle after obstacle. He was betrayed and forced to flee his home. His first copies of the New Testament were gathered up and burned. And on a voyage to print the book of Deuteronomy, he was shipwrecked and lost everything —"All his books, writings, and copies, his money and his time, and so was compelled to begin all again."[1]

Some obstacles were even closer to home. The religious world of his day stood against Tyndale in his quest to get the Bible to the people. That didn't stop him. Tyndale wrote, "Christ is with us until the world's end. Let his little flock be bold therefore. For if God be on our side, what matter maketh it who be against us, be they bishops, cardinals, popes, or whatsoever names they will?"[2]

William Tyndale was ultimately successful in printing the New Testament in English, and he also managed to print the first five books of the Old Testament. But he ended his life as a heroic martyr. While continuing to work on translating and printing the rest of the Bible, he was betrayed by a friend and imprisoned.

He was then convicted of heresy and executed by being strangled to death. Afterwards his body was burned at the stake. The last recorded words of his life were a prayer to see the Holy Scriptures spread throughout England.

"Lord! Open the king of England's eyes," he shouted while at the stake about to be killed.[3] What a brave man and courageous example of overcoming so many obstacles for the sake of the kingdom!

In what areas of your life can you be bold for Christ? You may not face the persecution that Tyndale faced, but is there some defeat or obstacle you need to overcome, even if it means a sacrifice on your part?

Dear almighty Lord, thank You that we have access to Your Holy Word. Forgive me for taking it for granted, and help me to approach it gratefully, knowing the lives that it cost to get it to me. Give me power today through Your words. In the name of Jesus Christ, amen.

PART 3

When You Need Courage in the Unknown

DAY 21

Discover God's Path for You

And who knows whether you have not come to the kingdom for such a time as this?

ESTHER 4:14 ESV

Do you ever wonder why you're in the season you're in? Do you sometimes get so wrapped up in projects and pre-occupations that you lose sight of what God is doing? Or have you ever felt disconnected and like God has abandoned you in the unknown?

God never leaves you. No matter what situation you're going through and what season of life you're in, God is always controlling and orchestrating the events in your life. Even during those times when the path is unclear or it seems like He's not there, God is present in every aspect of your life.

The book of Esther in the Old Testament is an example of the magnificent providence of God in one person's life. If you're

No matter what situation you're going through and what season of life you're in, God is always controlling and orchestrating the events in your life.

familiar with the story, perhaps you've noticed something remarkable: God is never mentioned in the book. Not even once. Yet Esther's story represents how God was at work to deliver the Jewish people from being destroyed.

Esther was the beautiful Jewish girl chosen out of many women to be the wife of King Xerxes I, the ruler over the great Persian empire. When an order called for all the Jews in the land to be executed, Esther risked her life to petition for the Jewish nation to be saved. In every part of Esther's gripping saga, we see God's hand working behind the scenes, even though He is never mentioned.

In the same way, God is present in your life. He pictured you before you were born. Every day of your life was detailed and written down—every moment documented—before you were even a day old (Psalm 139:16). Nothing catches Him off guard. This is a phenomenal and overwhelming thought. God has everything planned out—plans to take care of you and to give you a hopeful future (Jeremiah 29:11). Yet God still expects you to seek His will for your life.

The Lord planned your paths before you were born, yet as Paul wrote in Ephesians 5:17, "Don't act thoughtlessly, but understand what the Lord wants you to do" (NLT).

God had a very specific plan for Esther, and she fulfilled it, but she had to discover His path for her along the way. God has a plan for you, but you have to discover it. This comes from prayer, reading His Word, and listening to Him.

Look for God's guidance from the time you wake up until the moment you fall asleep. Even if He doesn't shout His presence, God is always present, and His plans for you are good.

Dear heavenly Father, I ask that You give me wisdom to discover the purpose You have for me. Thank You for orchestrating the events of my life and inviting me along on the path to discover Your good plan for me. I'm in awe that You call me Your masterpiece. Help me to remember that this present life is a vapor and to focus on the eternal. In Christ's name, amen.

DAY 22

Trust His Provision

"You cannot serve God and be enslaved to money. That is why I tell you not to worry about everyday life. . . . Can all your worries add a single moment to your life?"

MATTHEW 6:24–25, 27 NLT

J esus commands us not to worry. Why? Because God will never allow us to lack. David declared this in Psalm 37 when he wrote, "I was young and now I am old, yet I have never seen the righteous forsaken or their children begging bread" (v. 25 NIV).

But even knowing that, there are times in our lives when trusting God isn't easy.

In 1990, Lisa and I were launching the ministry and growing a young family. Though we had never been late on one bill, we had $300 to our name and were responsible for a $740-per-month house payment, $300-per-month car payment, and the expenses of our two infants. We didn't know where the money was going to come from, yet God had told me not to call churches or write letters in an attempt to get ministry invitations to speak for a fee.

In April of that year, things became very scarce. I didn't have any meetings scheduled, and I had been home for a full month. We were very low in our finances. Early one morning, I went out to pray. I was at my wit's end, and my time of prayer became more shouting out to God instead of quietly asking.

"Heavenly Father, I'm doing what You commanded me to do. If You don't open the doors and provide, I will go and get a job sacking groceries and tell everyone You didn't provide for us. But I'm not selling myself. If You have called me, You will open up doors. I give this concern totally to You."

Now, I'm not sure I would have made such a brash statement today, but there was something about the boldness of faith that pleased God, because shortly after that, a church in Michigan asked us to come preach for a four-day meeting. That four-day meeting turned into twenty-one services. It was a revival, and it was a great financial blessing. After that, my calendar was never scarce again.

Even though we live in turbulent and uncertain times, I encourage you to remember who your Provider is. It's not your employer, not your paycheck, not the stock market, and not the economy. God is your Provider.

Dear heavenly Father, forgive me for the times I worry about provision. You care about the birds of the air, and You care much more for me. I will trust You for providing anything I need. In Jesus' name, amen.

Obey God Completely

"Now I know that you fear God, because you have
not withheld from me your son, your only son."

GENESIS 22:12 NIV

Abraham had a holy fear of God. We see this clearly in
Genesis 22, when God asked Abraham to make a great sacrifice. The story goes something like this:

When Abraham was old, God came to him one night.

"Abraham!"

"Yes, Lord. I'm here."

"I want you to take your son, the one you love so much and
waited twenty-five years for, and I want you to go on a three-day
journey and sacrifice him for Me."

Can you imagine how hard that must have been? How could
God ask something so appalling, so mind-numbing, from His
devoted follower? God didn't even give Abraham a reason!

I can only imagine what Abraham was thinking.

*Am I hearing this correctly? Is this a bad dream? How can this
be? I love my son—I can't put Isaac to death. Kings and nations are*

promised to come through him. How can this promise be fulfilled if I kill him?

However, despite his lack of understanding, we read, "Early the next morning Abraham got up and loaded his donkey" (Genesis 22:3 NIV). He didn't have answers or reasons or logic, but he chose to obey God anyway.

Abraham didn't wait months or weeks or even days to act on God's request. He acted *the next morning.*

Even though it would have been the most painful thing for him to do, he obeyed God. Isaac was the fulfillment of God's promise in his life. Abraham had waited patiently for more than twenty-five years to see God's promise come to pass—and then he was asked to lay it all down, and God didn't even give him an explanation. Still, he obeyed.

We all know the end of the story—God spared Isaac and delivered on all His promises—but Abraham didn't know how it would end. All he knew was that he feared God and trusted Him completely, even when it didn't make sense to his natural mind.

Abraham went to the mountain and built the altar, then he took Isaac up on the altar and raised his knife, ready to put his precious son to death—when all of a sudden, an angel appeared and told him to stop. "Do not lay your hand on the lad, or do anything to him; for now I know that you fear God" (v. 12).

Did you catch that? God wanted to know that Abraham *feared Him.* He wanted to know this enough to put Abraham through an ultimate test of obedience. And Abraham's response proved that he did fear God.

Obedience is the outward evidence of the fear of the Lord. When we fear God, we will obey Him—even if it hurts, even if we don't understand, even if we can't see the benefit. God will never test us in the exact way He tested Abraham—but He might ask for a great sacrifice that feels impossible to make. Will you obey Him?

What is God asking you to do in obedience? Your obedience to God will open the doors to His blessing and position you to step into all He has for you.

Dear Jehovah-Jireh, my Lord and Provider, give me the strength to obey You even when it doesn't make sense, even when it hurts, and even if I don't see a benefit. Forgive me for not prioritizing Your desires and commands over everything else in my life. I ask for the holy fear and grace to obey you completely. In Jesus' name, amen.

Some Great Reward

Always continue to fear the LORD.
You will be rewarded for this; your
hope will not be disappointed.

PROVERBS 23:17–18 NLT

We need courageous faith when we face the unknown, bold faith to live for a future we can't map out perfectly. But God promises that our hopes will not be disappointed, that we will be rewarded if we keep fearing Him.

God has a great reward waiting for us if only we will seek Him. Not a worldly reward of fame and fortune and fun, but one much greater. What exactly is that reward?

Moses asked that very same question as he waited in faith.

For forty years, Moses grew up and lived with tremendous wealth in Pharaoh's house in Egypt—the finest foods, fashionable clothing, the best material possessions, and any desirable pleasure. He lived in a spectacular home; no one on earth was more wealthy or powerful than his grandfather, the pharaoh. Yet look what Hebrews 11:24–28 says in *The Message*:

By faith, Moses, when grown, refused the privileges of the Egyptian royal house. He chose a hard life with God's people rather than an opportunistic soft life of sin with the oppressors. He valued suffering in the Messiah's camp far greater than Egyptian wealth because he was looking ahead, anticipating the payoff. By an act of faith, he turned his heel on Egypt, indifferent to the king's blind rage. He had his eye on the One no eye can see, and kept right on going.

Moses could have stayed in the palace and attempted to serve God in safety and in luxury, but he knew there was more in God's plan for him—much more, in fact. So he chose to walk away from everything that was safe, comfortable, and known. Moses knew there was a call of God on his life at forty years of age. Of course, it took another forty long years before he found out exactly what he was seeking. But first Moses needed to be refined and prepared for what God had in store for him.

Look at what Moses ultimately desired as his greatest reward. When God instructed him to round up His people and take them to the promised land, saying He had assigned an angel to guide them out, God also declared, "But I will not go with you myself" (Exodus 33:3 GNT). The Israelites had longed for the promised land for generations. Yet look at Moses' reply to God's offer: "If you don't personally go with us, don't make us leave this place" (Exodus 33:15 NLT).

We need
courageous faith
when we face
the unknown,
bold faith to live
for a future we
can't map out
perfectly.

Moses essentially revealed that if he had to choose between God's presence and God's blessings, he would rather take God's presence, even in the discomfort of the desert. Moses desired to be as close and intimate with God as he could be. This was Moses' coveted reward, and God gave it to him.

What is your great reward? What calling does God have for you? Are you willing to leave the "palaces" or places of comfort in your life to seek out God and where He's calling you?

Dear heavenly Father, I know You don't just want me to speak my faith but to act on it. Please give me courage and boldness to live in a way that glorifies Jesus as I journey into the unknown future. You are my great reward, and no one can take that from me. In Jesus' name, amen.

Pray Courageously

And we are confident that he
hears us whenever we ask for
anything that pleases him.

1 JOHN 5:14 NLT

In the middle of the night, a mother prays for her son, pleading for God to save his soul. He has spent his youth following his desires, searching for answers while living a promiscuous lifestyle. But the mother never gave up hope, as her son would one day write: "My mother, your faithful servant, wept more for me than mothers weep over their children's dead bodies. By that spirit of faith which she had from you, she saw my death, and you graciously heard her, O Lord."[1]

For fifteen years this woman, Monica, prayed and wept and fasted for her son, Aurelius Augustinus Hipponensis, who would eventually be known as Augustine of Hippo.

Augustine, an errant youth who had searched long and hard for meaning in all the wrong places, eventually was confronted with the truth he had been searching for. He stood in terror, unable to escape from himself and the mess he had made with his life. After seeing the faith conversion of two men, he turned to his close friend in shock.

"What is the matter with us? What is the meaning of this story? These men have none of our education, yet they stand up and storm the gates of heaven while we, for all our learning, lie here groveling in this world of flesh and blood!"

Augustine could have easily run away from God's tugging at his heart and gone back to his fleshly desires and distractions, but instead he found himself drawn to Scripture. He opened the Bible to Paul's letter to the Romans and read the following: "Let us behave decently, as in the daytime, not in carousing and drunkenness, not in sexual immorality and debauchery, not in dissension and jealousy. Rather, clothe yourselves with the Lord Jesus Christ, and do not think about how to gratify the desires of the flesh" (Romans 13:13–14 NIV).

He didn't need to read any more. In that instant, his heart was filled with faith in Christ. Any doubt he had carried disappeared.

Augustine's conversion story had a huge impact on Christian history, and he became one of the fathers of the church and one of the most influential theologians of all time.

His story doesn't just reveal that God can redeem anyone. It also shows the unwavering confidence of a mother's faith.

Courageous faith doesn't always come in the form of public conversations and actions. It also comes in silence and solitude, with a heart open to our heavenly Father and asking for His mercy. We are promised God will answer our prayers of faith; however, the "when" and "how" are up to Him. All you have to do is continue to ask in faith before Him.

Dear gracious and loving Father, You know everything and hear every prayer of faith offered up to You. Thank You for listening to me and answering my prayers in Your perfect ways. I know You are always listening, and I'm so grateful for this. So lead me now as I call upon You in confidence. In Jesus' name, amen.

DAY 26

Wait Patiently in the Wilderness

Wait patiently for the LORD. Be brave and courageous. Yes, wait patiently for the LORD.

PSALM 27:14 NLT

D oes God feel miles away? Do you appear to be going in the opposite direction of your dreams and the promises you were certain He'd made to you? Do you feel like God's presence seems to be diminishing instead of growing? Maybe you even feel unloved and ignored.

All believers have felt like this before. We all spend time in the wilderness. If we are to be like Jesus, our character must develop, and many times this happens in the dry places. It's a common place for sincere followers of Christ to find themselves in. It might feel like God has abandoned you, but in reality, He is close at hand, having promised never to leave nor forsake you (Hebrews 13:5).

Never forget that many of God's saints have been forged in the wilderness.

Abraham, a wealthy man from Ur who lived in comfort, was asked by God to leave everything behind to find a new promised land. He and Sarah ended up on a long journey with many lonely nights in the desert.

There was also Moses, who spent forty years on the back side of the desert. Joseph, who was stuck in slavery and then Pharaoh's dungeon. David, who hid in caves. John the Baptist, who lived in the deserts of Judea, wearing animal skins and eating insects. Jesus, who after being filled with the Spirit was immediately led into the wilderness for forty days. John the apostle, who was exiled to the deserted island of Patmos.

All of these heroes of the faith went through a wilderness season as a place of preparation for the next phase of what God was calling them to do for the kingdom. So often when God shows us great things that He intends to do through us in the future, He first leads us into a wilderness to prepare us.

God has a plan for your wilderness season and doesn't intend for you to spend longer there than necessary, but it's ultimately up to you if it will be extended. The wilderness is merely a place of preparation before God leads us into our promise. The more we press into God through surrender, obedience, and trust, the sooner we'll step into all He has for us.

If you're stuck in a wilderness, believe that God is still there with you. He has brought you into that place so that you may know what is in your heart. The wilderness is where your faith is refined and your character developed.

Do not quit in your pursuit of Him. Do not give up. Wait patiently in the wilderness. Keep the vision that He's given you, no matter how the circumstances appear.

Dear heavenly Father, forgive me for doubting Your constant presence. Help me to be patient when I don't hear You, and help me to always pursue Your will in my life, even in the dry seasons and in the wilderness. I trust You are preparing me and refining me. In Jesus' name, amen.

Direction in the Desert

**He will fulfill the desire of those who fear Him;
He also will hear their cry and save them.**

PSALM 145:19

Do you ever find yourself uncertain of God's plan for you? Maybe you have unmet desires or dreams that have been waiting for years, decades even. Maybe you've followed God's call into unknown places, but now you're waiting and feel stuck—and you can't see the way forward.

It's not easy to be patient and wait on God. When Moses fled Egypt, he went to a place called Midian where he spent forty years taking care of sheep (Exodus 2). He didn't go straight to the promised land or lead the Israelites out of Egypt right away. Instead, he went from being a prince, a general, and an educated man at the very top of society to a humble and lowly shepherd—for decades.

The path might not always make sense to us at the moment, but God's path is always the right one. The long, winding, and uncertain route is sometimes what it takes for God to shape us into the men and women He wants us to be.

The long, winding, and uncertain route is sometimes what it takes for God to shape us into the men and women He wants us to be.

He may lead us into the wilderness for a while, but there is always a purpose there. There is *always* a purpose.

Moses spent forty years in his wilderness until God suddenly revealed Himself at Mount Sinai in the burning bush. Moses responded by saying, "I will now turn aside and see this great sight" (Exodus 3:3). He was given the unbelievable opportunity to meet God and experience His presence, which only could have happened at that time and in that place. After that, nothing would ever be the same. His path and direction soon became clear.

There is a purpose for every season—even the wilderness. What direction are you looking for today? God will reveal Himself to you in fresh ways, even in your dry times, if you continue to seek Him.

Dear heavenly Father, You know the season I am in, and You can see my heart. You know my desires and You hear my cries. You have things for me that only You can bring to pass. Show me my purpose today and equip me for it. In Jesus' name, amen.

DAY 28

Intimacy or Idolatry

My heart has heard you say, "Come and talk with me." And my heart responds, "Lord, I am coming."

PSALM 27:8 NLT

When we have to wait on God in the unknown, it can be tempting to take matters into our own hands. We want to fast-track the journey and get right to the promises, right to the good stuff.

In this way, our church today very much resembles the people Moses brought to Mount Sinai. They were promised deliverance, and God displayed His power triumphantly with the parting of the Red Sea and the destruction of their captors.

But when Moses delivered them out of Egypt, they didn't go right to the promised land. Remember what Moses told Pharaoh: "Let my people go, so they can worship me in the wilderness" (Exodus 7:16 NLT). He said this *seven* times. The promised land is never referred to.

Moses had to bring the people into the wilderness first. He took them to where he had met God at the burning bush at Mount

Sinai. He wanted them to encounter the presence of God too. Unfortunately, the Israelites only wanted the promises of God.

We know the story. When Moses brought the people to meet God, they reeled back in terror. Not with the fear of God, but with the fear of losing their own lives! So they told Moses to act as an intermediary between them and God. While Moses was gone on the mountain, the people became impatient and coerced Moses' brother, Aaron, to make a golden calf that they could worship. They made their own version of God and they chose to worship it. They didn't deny that Jehovah had delivered them out of slavery; they just changed His image into a manageable deity that would give them what their flesh craved.

Many Christians do this today. They call Jesus their Lord but they don't follow Him. Instead, they follow their own will. They don't wait on the Lord's timing but instead act for their own needs. They pick only the passages of Scripture that they want to obey.

Who is the Jesus that you follow? Is He one who thinks, talks, and walks like the rest of the world? This knockoff Jesus will only lead you to where the golden calf led the Israelites: Nowhere. A barren place of wandering.

God delivered the Israelites out of Egypt to bring them to Himself, to be their God and for them to be His people. God always desires intimacy with us.

What idols are in the way of intimacy with God for you today? Can you recognize them? Can you call them by name? Identify them, destroy them, and run to God!

Dear heavenly Father, forgive me for the times I've changed Your image into a false "God" who would give me what my selfish desires craved. I repent. Please give me the strength to worship the true Jesus and not some knockoff. I desire intimacy with You above all. I ask this in Jesus' name, amen.

Build a Firm Foundation

Praise the LORD! Blessed is the man who fears the LORD, who delights greatly in His commandments.

PSALM 112:1

The wise man built his house upon the rock, the wise man built his house upon the rock!"

Can you hear the song so many children learn to sing in Sunday school? While it's a simple melody, the truth in those words is profound. The song is based on the conclusion of Jesus' famous Sermon on the Mount, and the words focus on the strength of a person's foundation.

Both men in Jesus' story appeared to have a well-built house. Yet when the storms came, the strength of each house's foundation was truly tested and seen for what it was. While it's easy for us to think we are the wise builder, we shouldn't be so quick to assume this.

Did you know the difference between sand and rock is far more subtle than you may think? One is simply small particles of the other, conforming to whatever presses against it. This is an example of what many people do today in our culture.

We know the value of reading the Word of God. However, there are more and more people who are focusing on the parts of Scripture they find comfortable while ignoring sections that are hard to live out or might offend others. Jesus was talking about this in His illustration about the wise man and the foolish man. Both men heard God's Word, but only one of them actually heeded the words.

In essence, there are some people who fear God and tremble at His Word, securing themselves on a firm foundation. And there are others who don't fear Him nor tremble at His Word—they delight in hearing, but when adhering interferes with personal desire, they ignore instruction and consequently build themselves a faulty foundation.

The apostle James gave us a warning: "Do not merely listen to the word, and so deceive yourselves. Do what it says" (James 1:22 NIV). God has given us all the things we need to live a godly life. Scripture is full of great promises. "These are the promises that enable you to share his divine nature and escape the world's corruption caused by human desires" (2 Peter 1:4 NLT). These are the promises that help us build a solid foundation.

Dear heavenly Father, help me to not only be a hearer of Your Word but also a doer. I know I need to build a firm foundation to protect me during the storms in life. Thank You for revealing Yourself and Your promises to me in Scripture. In Jesus' name, amen.

Trust in the Lord

But blessed are those who trust in the Lᴏʀᴅ and have made the Lᴏʀᴅ their hope and confidence.

JEREMIAH 17:7 ɴʟᴛ

Courage moves us forward despite the fears that can come with uncertain situations. Confidence in ourselves won't get us far. Confidence in Christ, however, gives us the courage to face any adversity that may come.

I was twenty-three years old when Lisa and I got married. Two weeks after I turned twenty-four, I walked away from a very good position as a mechanical engineer on a multimillion-dollar government Navy project. God had directed me to my life calling to preach the gospel. My first step toward doing this was driving a van to take care of the personal needs of my pastor and his family.

With my new job I took a significant pay cut. For four and a half years, Lisa and I lived hand to mouth, yet we watched as God always provided for us.

It was during this time that a man offered for me to go to the Philippines and preach with him. The plane ticket was two thousand dollars. "I'll pay half of your ticket," he said. "You believe God for the other half."

A week before leaving, I still didn't have the money to pay for it, and Lisa approached me.

"John," she said. "Please tell me you're not going to get on that plane if God doesn't give us a thousand dollars."

"I give you my word I won't do it."

Even though I had shared the Philippines outreach opportunity with people in the large church we attended, nobody had stepped in to help. It was not looking good.

The wealthiest man in the church volunteered to drive me to the airport, yet the Monday morning I was supposed to leave, a Bible school student showed up at my apartment instead. He explained that the wealthy man couldn't drive me after all and had called him to see if he could help out.

On the drive to the airport, I faced my reality. I only had twenty-five dollars in my wallet, and I had promised Lisa I wouldn't get on that plane if the ticket wasn't paid for.

You gotta stick this thing out, I told myself.

I figured the worst-case scenario would be that I would watch my plane take off and then use the twenty-five dollars to get a cab home.

Back in those days, guests could walk into airline terminals with passengers, so the student insisted on accompanying me to my gate to help with my luggage. When we arrived at the gate, he dropped my bags.

"I heard this past Wednesday that you were going on this trip," the student said. "And the Holy Spirit told me you needed a thousand dollars for the ticket."

I had never told anybody that specific amount. Not a single person. Yet that was the exact figure he said.

"I stayed up half the night on Wednesday arguing with God," the student continued. "I finally said, 'God, if You make a miraculous way for me to give it to him, I'll do it.'"

The young man then explained that the businessman had called him the following evening to ask him to drive me to the airport. When he was asked, the student almost fell out of his bed.

"You've got the money," he told me. "Now get on the plane."

That was one of the most life-changing and significant trips of my entire life. I remember calling Lisa from the airport afterward.

"Can you believe this absolute miracle?" I asked her.

That one incident has given me the courage to believe God for millions of dollars to help pastors and leaders in developing and persecuted nations. We go from faith to faith, but we have to start on the small things first.

Miracles do happen. We just have to find the courage to meet up with them.

Think about a time when God answered something in an unexpected way for you. Then consider the ways you need to trust in God to provide for the challenges you face today.

Dear heavenly Father, I ask for faith to receive Your wisdom as I read Your Word, pray, and hear godly counsel from those who fear You. Give me the strength to believe and obey, even if it doesn't make sense. In Jesus' name I pray, amen.

PART 4

When You Need Courage to Live with Bold Faith

DAY 31

Speak Out

There was a man sent from God, whose name was John. This man came for a witness, to bear witness of the Light, that all through him might believe. He was not that Light, but was sent to bear witness of that Light.

JOHN 1:6–8

If cancel culture had existed in the days before Jesus began His ministry, the first person to be deleted would have been John the Baptist. He never held back in telling people to repent and get ready for the coming of the Savior. People came from all directions to hear him preach; those who confessed their sins were baptized by John in the Jordan River. But when the Pharisees and Sadducees showed up wanting to be baptized, he called them out.

"'Brood of snakes! What do you think you're doing slithering down here to the river? Do you think a little water on your snakeskins is going to make any difference? It's your life that must change, not your skin!'" (Matthew 3:7–8 MSG).

Nothing about John the Baptist fit with his culture: he looked wild and unruly and lived off the land, eating locusts and wild honey. Yet he spoke with sincerity and truth.

Do you ever fear speaking with that same kind of honesty? There was a time when people who disagreed with one another could still have healthy conversations. But now we are ostracized and attacked for sharing opinions and beliefs, especially when they don't conform to popular culture. We often remain silent.

All of us are ambassadors for Christ. And like John the Baptist, we can't just tell people what they want to hear. If we truly love them, we must speak the truth. Yes, we should do this in a spirit of love, but we must remember to *do it*.

The apostle Paul also spoke the truth, as he shared in Acts: "I never shrank back from telling you what you needed to hear, either publicly or in your homes. I have had one message for Jews and Greeks alike—the necessity of repenting from sin and turning to God, and of having faith in our Lord Jesus" (20:20–21 NLT).

Don't shrink back today. Like John the Baptist, you bear witness to Jesus, the Light of the world.

Dear heavenly Father, help me never to hesitate to share the message of Jesus Christ to the world. Let me be a shining light in this dark world. In Jesus' name, amen.

Don't Give Up

That you may walk (live and conduct yourselves) in a manner worthy of the Lord, fully pleasing to Him and desiring to please Him in all things, bearing fruit in every good work.

COLOSSIANS 1:10 AMPC

Do you ever see the evil in today's world and feel convicted to speak out, yet remain silent? It's easy to stay quiet in these days of cancel culture and online vitriol. Yet as believers, we can't be mute audience members watching the insanity and injustices of our world. We need to proclaim the hope of Jesus Christ whenever we can—especially when there is darkness or despair.

William Wilberforce never held back when it came to voicing the truth God had put in his heart. As a young member of Parliament in Great Britain, he gave his life to Christ in his twenties and devoted himself to living out his faith in a very public way. Living in the late 1700s at the height of the slave trade, Wilberforce saw the wickedness of slavery and made up his mind to be an advocate for ending it.

As believers,
we can't be
mute audience
members
watching the
insanity and
injustices of
our world.

"I take courage," Wilberforce said in his abolition speech in 1789, "I determine to forget all my other fears, and I march forward with a firmer step in the full assurance that my cause will bear me out."[1]

For years Wilberforce did just that, marching forward in Parliament to introduce bills for abolition, but none of them got through. Still, he never gave up. After twenty years of fighting, the bill was carried by a surprising majority in the House of Commons, which finally abolished the slave trade in the British West Indies.

The dedication William Wilberforce demonstrated could only have come from the faith he carried. In the introduction to his book *Real Christianity*, Wilberforce wrote about his faith:

> I am disturbed when I see the majority of so-called Christians having such little understanding of the real nature of the faith they profess. Faith is a subject of such importance that we should not ignore it because of the distractions or the hectic pace of our lives. Life as we know it, with all its ups and downs, will soon be over. We all will give an accounting to God of how we have lived.[2]

How do you live out your faith day by day? How can you share your Christian walk with others even if that puts you at odds with them? How can you, as William Wilberforce declared, "boldly assert the cause of Christ in an age when so many, who bear the name of Christians, are ashamed of Him"?[3]

Dear Holy Father, I praise You for Your glory and majesty. Help me to live in a manner worthy of You, pleasing to You. Help me to bear fruit and fight injustice with Your truth. Please keep before me that I bear the name of Christ, and give me a bolder faith. In Jesus' name, amen.

DAY 33

Love What God Loves

All who fear the Lord will hate evil. Therefore, I hate pride and arrogance, corruption and perverse speech.

PROVERBS 8:13 NLT

When was the last time you felt completely powerless? Maybe it was in a job or a relationship? Perhaps everything you were trying to do failed, and every solution got you nowhere.

There was a time in my life when I was preaching but my words felt so lifeless. I had been asking God to put some strength behind my words. Every day I woke up at 4:45 a.m. so I could be outside at 5:00 to pray. I would pray for an hour and a half or so every single morning. But I didn't see much change.

I grew frustrated, and one day I called out to God: "I read Your Bible. I pray for an hour and a half to two hours every day. I'm living a godly life. So why isn't there a stronger anointing on my life?"

The Holy Spirit immediately replied, *Because you tolerate sin, not only in your life, but in the lives of others.*

He then told me to read Hebrews 1 to hear what God the Father says about the authority of Jesus. I began to read. When I got to verses 8–9, the Holy Spirit told me to stop and read it again: "Your throne, O God, is forever and ever; a scepter of righteousness is the scepter of Your kingdom. You have loved righteousness and hated lawlessness; therefore God, Your God, has anointed You . . . more than Your companions."

I understood the part about loving righteousness. Every Christian loves righteousness, or aspires to loving it. But what about hating lawlessness? That part exposed my lack of conviction.

Suddenly, I began to see what the Holy Spirit was telling me. If I learned to hate sin the way Jesus hated sin, I would see the anointing of God increase in my life. There were sins I was tolerating, looking over, disliking but not hating, not only in my life but in the lives of other believers who were close to me.

Let me further clarify so there's no misunderstanding. It bothers me when people say, "I fear God, and that's why I hate people who are living in sin like that." Because here's the truth: You don't fear God. You don't fear Him at all. Because you hate what He loves. God so loved every single one of us that He gave His only Son to save us.

God hates *sin*. He hates anything that undoes us because He passionately loves us, every single person on this planet.

When we fear God, we take on His heart. We want to be as close to Him as we can. The fear of the Lord is a gift from our loving heavenly Father that protects us from departing from Him. The moment we develop a tolerance for sin, rather than a hate for it, is the moment we begin our departure from Him.

Dear heavenly Father, help me to love all people, because I know You love all people. But also help me hate the sin that You hate. Open my eyes to the sins I tolerate, the sins that Jesus gave His life to free us from. In Jesus' name, amen.

Swim Against the Tide

Unfailing love and faithfulness make atonement
for sin. By fearing the Lord, people avoid evil.

PROVERBS 16:6 NLT

In June 1971, Billy Graham delivered his famous sermon titled "Who Is Jesus" during his Chicago Crusade. In an event lasting ten days, nearly twelve thousand individuals made a decision to follow Christ. Graham warned his listeners about making such a decision:

> I think in many ways, it's easier not to be a Christian in this world because the devil may leave you alone. The moment you receive Christ as Savior, you're in for it, unless you live on your knees and stay in the Scriptures and keep your guard up and wear your spiritual armor at all times. Because if you let down even one day as a Christian, you're in trouble. The moment you receive Christ, you see, all the world is going this way. You turn around and start against the tide as a Christian. And that's hard.[1]

One of the earliest heroes of the faith displayed this with his life. Joseph was Abraham's great-grandson, and God showed Joseph in a dream that he would one day be a great ruler, even reigning over his own brothers. But right after receiving this promise, Joseph was thrown into a pit, and he spent the next decade in slavery and at least two additional years in a dungeon. Yet not once do we ever see evidence of Joseph dropping his guard or going the easy route.

Joseph didn't abandon his hope in God.

Joseph didn't forget the dream God gave him.

Joseph feared God.

This fear of God is perhaps evidenced the most when Joseph avoided temptation and didn't yield to Potiphar's wife when she tried to seduce him. He stated, "No one here has more authority than I do. He [Potiphar] has held back nothing from me except you, because you are his wife. How could I do such a wicked thing? It would be a great sin against God" (Genesis 39:9 NLT).

Joseph's obedience to God landed him in a dark dungeon, but he remained strong. For more than twelve years, he lived in a spiritual desert where it seemed nothing was going his way. But there was a reservoir deep inside of him from which Joseph drew. This reservoir provided the courage he needed to obey God in tough and silent times.

Joseph kept his spiritual armor on and refused to be separated from the Lord. He was wise in his behavior because he feared God. "The fear of the LORD is the instruction of wisdom"

It's hard to be a Christian in today's world. Keep that spiritual armor on at all times.

(Proverbs 15:33). This wisdom caused Joseph to eventually shine brightly in Egypt when his virtues were revealed to an entire pagan nation.

The reality is that it's hard to be a Christian in today's world. Every single day, we have to "live in the Scriptures and keep [our] guard up," as Billy Graham stated. Keep that spiritual armor on at all times. You will need it.

Dear Father, creator of all things and ruler over everything, thank You for giving us the tools we need to stay equipped in our faith. Help me not to let down my guard today, in big ways and small ways. Help me fear You and not this world. In Jesus Christ's name, amen.

Walk Through the Fire

> "If you try to hang on to your life, you
> will lose it. But if you give up your life
> for my sake, you will save it."
>
> MATTHEW 16:25 NLT

History has recorded the heroism of Joan of Arc, the peasant girl who led the French army to a victory and was later burned at the stake for heresy when she was only nineteen years old. There is another heroic Joan, one who should be celebrated in the history of the Christian faith. Her name was Joan Mathurin.

Some of the earliest known Christians were the Vaudois, who were believers of Jesus Christ located in the valleys of the Alps. They founded churches and spread the gospel throughout present-day Italy, France, Germany, Spain, and Poland. They were heavily persecuted, "branded and burnt as heretics,"[1] and their faith and obedience made them instrumental to key figures such as John Wycliffe and others during the Protestant Reformation that came after them.

One such martyr was Joan Mathurin. In 1560, after her husband was arrested for conducting family prayers and refused to renounce his faith, he was scheduled to be burned alive. Joan visited him in prison, not just because she loved him but to encourage him to be firm in his faith up to the end. When the magistrates saw her actions, they ordered her to tell her husband to obey them. Instead, she remained strong and proclaimed the name of Jesus Christ.

"Heretical she devil," they called her, telling her she should fear dying and being put in the flames with her husband.

"I fear Him who is able to cast both body and soul into a more terrible fire than that of your billets," Joan stated.[2]

The next day, Joan and her husband were led to the public square, tied to wooden stakes, and burned alive. Neither ever denied Jesus despite the unspeakable terror of their deaths.

Can you imagine being murdered for your faith? It's one thing to be publicly shamed or privately bullied for your Christian beliefs, but what would you do if standing up for Jesus Christ meant being put to death? How strong would you be?

Christian martyrs like Joan Mathurin and her husband are examples for us to study and ponder. What made their faith so strong? How were they able to remain so dedicated and courageous in the face of persecution? Paul's words to Timothy shed light on their strength's source: "My son, be strong in the grace that is in Christ Jesus" (2 Timothy 2:1). His free grace not only forgives you but empowers you to stand firm in His truth no matter the opposition.

Dear Father, please open my heart and help me to have a faith that withstands all attacks. Help me to value eternal things. I long to obey Your Word, even if I'm persecuted for my beliefs or obedience. In Jesus' name, amen.

DAY 36

Speak God's Truth

No wonder people everywhere
fear him. All who are wise
show him reverence.

JOB 37:24 NLT

A few years ago, I got on a plane and heard the Holy Spirit tell me to open the Bible to Job 32.

Oh, no. . . . Not Job.

I'll be honest. There are two books of the Bible I approach with a bit of apprehension and find myself really leaning into for the wisdom of the Holy Spirit: Job and Ecclesiastes. I actually like the book of Revelation, but Job is a challenge for me.

But when you hear the Spirit speak, you listen. So I opened my Bible and began to read. At this part of the book, Job had been sorely tested and had suffered greatly. After trying to make sense of his overwhelming loss, he fell into despair, and despite his friends' counsel, he felt abandoned and confused.

But then a wise young preacher named Elihu, who had been silent in hopes of hearing wisdom from the older men (Job and his three friends), finally spoke out. He spoke boldly and didn't hold back speaking truth to Job.

"I'm so fed up with listening to this," Elihu basically said to the others offering counsel. "You guys have not been speaking wisdom. I'm younger, so I waited to speak, thinking it was going to come from you."

Elihu proceeded to speak the truth to Job and the others with no apologies. The final words he spoke to Job and his friends were, "No wonder people everywhere fear him. All who are wise show him reverence" (Job 37:24 NLT).

In the very next verse, the Lord came in a whirlwind and made His presence known.

After reading these words, I heard God speak to me on that plane: *John, did you notice that My presence did not manifest while Job or those three men spoke? It wasn't until somebody spoke the truth unapologetically, with a loving heart, that I made My presence known. There are myriad churches in this country that are misrepresenting Me, and My presence is not manifesting.*

I was convicted to my core.

Throughout church history, Christians have been stoned and put on racks and excommunicated. But today? We have church leaders doing shots with celebrities and reducing their calling to that of life coaches to the famous. Their goal is now to inspire rather than to speak the Word of God in love.

I'm not trying to be overly critical. And with four sons and daughters-in-law, I understand the desire to be relevant. I'm okay with cool as long as it doesn't compromise truth. But nowadays in the church, community and coolness often trump the lordship of Jesus. And this is destroying people. They are leaving the faith in droves. Why? Because we aren't teaching, rebuking, and exhorting with the truth of God's Word. Because there is a lack of the fear of the Lord.

When leaders speak what God speaks, His presence will manifest!

Gracious heavenly Father, forgive me when I approach You with too casual of an attitude. Help me not lose sight of who You are. Help me to always speak Your truth to others. In Jesus' name I pray, amen.

Comprehend His Love

How precious also are Your thoughts
to me, O God! How great is the sum of
them! If I should count them, they would
be more in number than the sand

PSALM 139:17–18

What if we lived every moment of the day truly believing these words King David wrote in this psalm? What if we believed the truth that God's thoughts about us are more than all the granules of sand covering the earth?

Science and math enthusiasts tell us that, depending on the size and how tightly packed, there are approximately five hundred million to a billion granules of sand in *one cubic square foot* of beach. Knowing this fact, it's hard to even comprehend the incredible amount of sand on the last beach you visited. Add up every granule of sand on the planet, and you still won't have the number of thoughts God has about you!

Jesus speaks of how much God pays attention to us in Luke 12:6–7:

"What's the price of two or three pet canaries? Some loose change, right? But God never overlooks a single one. And he pays even greater attention to you, down to the last detail—even numbering the hairs on your head! So don't be intimidated by all this bully talk. You're worth more than a million canaries." (MSG)

God so deeply cherishes you that He knows the number of hairs on your head. It's estimated that most humans have on average 100,000 hairs on their scalp. If you put 10,000 people in a room, do you think you could determine which one has 99,569 hairs? Even if you guessed correctly, you'd be wrong in minutes because the average person loses fifty to one hundred hairs per day. God knows our exact number at any given moment.

God doesn't just think about us and know us more than we can comprehend. His love for us is unfathomable. Jesus shares this startling statement in a prayer: "The world will know that you [God] sent me [Jesus Christ] and that you love them as much as you love me" (John 17:23 NLT).

The depth of God's love and the value He places on you is incomprehensible, and that should give you courage to live out your faith boldly. If His love is so great, what is there that you cannot overcome? For this reason we are told, "There is no fear

God's love
should give
you courage
to live out
your faith
boldly.

in love; but perfect love casts out fear" (1 John 4:18). Consider this throughout your day, and boldly love and meet the needs of those you encounter.

Dear heavenly Father, I can't grasp how much You know me, how much You care for me. You know every hair on my head, and You loved me enough to send Your Son, Jesus, to die in my place. Help me to comprehend Your love and live my faith boldly. In Jesus' name, amen.

Continue to Follow

In the same way, when you obey me you should say, "We are unworthy servants who have simply done our duty."

LUKE 17:10 NLT

Follow me."

These are the first words Jesus spoke to Simon Peter while standing on the shore of the Sea of Galilee. Peter and Andrew were fishing when Jesus called out to them and said, "Come, follow me, and I will show you how to fish for people!" (Matthew 4:19 NLT).

Years later, everything changed. Even after following Jesus throughout His ministry, Peter watched Him get arrested and soon denied he ever knew Him in the first place. Jesus remained obedient to God's will and died a criminal's death on the cross. By the time the angel of the Lord appeared to Mary Magdalene at the tomb to share the news of Jesus' resurrection, Peter had been shaken to the point of giving up.

"Now go and tell his disciples, including Peter, that Jesus is going ahead of you to Galilee. You will see him there, just as he told you before he died" (Mark 16:7 NLT).

The angel singled Peter out because the disciple was submerged in guilt and grief. When Peter finally saw Jesus after fishing on the sea of Tiberias, the Lord encouraged him.

"'I tell you the truth, when you were young, you were able to do as you liked; you dressed yourself and went wherever you wanted to go. But when you are old, you will stretch out your hands, and others will dress you and take you where you don't want to go'" (John 21:18 NLT).

I believe Jesus was telling Peter, "You may have failed Me before, but there is coming a day when you will face your greatest fear and be victorious."

Peter may have denied Jesus, but he ultimately followed Him to the end. Peter understood it was impossible to fulfill the call of God on his life in his own ability. He knew the antidote to the fear of man was to live in reverent fear of God (1 Peter 1:13–17).

Peter would be tested again, but the next time he would be victorious. Peter obeyed Jesus and continued to follow Him. He also fulfilled what he once previously vowed to Jesus: he died before denying Jesus. History reveals that Peter was crucified upside down after the disciple insisted he was unworthy to die in the same manner that Jesus died.

We can make mistakes and fail in our lives, but Peter is an example of how to face our fears and weaknesses with the grace of Jesus Christ. Peter's life is an example of finishing strong.

Dear heavenly Father, apart from Jesus, I am indeed an unworthy servant before Your eyes. I'm forever thankful to You for making me worthy in Him. Forgive me for not obeying Your commands and not heeding Your words when under the pressure of hostility from others. You are worthy to follow. In Jesus' name, amen.

DAY 39

Spend Time in the Word

**Your word is a lamp to guide my feet
and a light for my path.**

PSALM 119:105 NLT

Evangelist, publisher, and the founder of the Moody Church in Chicago, D. L. Moody knew the value of studying the Scriptures. In his book *Pleasure & Profit in Bible Study,* he said this:

> When I pray, I talk to God, but when I read the Bible, God is talking to me; and it is really more important that God should speak to me than that I should speak to Him. I believe we should know better how to pray if we knew our Bibles better. What is an army good for if they don't know how to use their weapons?[1]

Don't ever doubt it: Scripture renews your mind. It is a map to guide you in your daily walk with God. It's an instructional manual for your life.

According to a study by the Center of Bible Engagement, those who read God's Word four times a week are:

- 30 percent less likely to feel lonely
- 32 percent less likely to be angry
- 40 percent less likely to be bitter
- 57 percent less likely to suffer from alcoholism
- 59 percent less likely to view pornography
- 60 percent less likely to feel spiritually stagnant[2]

Moreover, it's never been easier to read Scripture. I can read and listen to the Bible from my phone and from my iPad, but when it comes to time alone with the Lord, I still prefer a physical Bible in front of me. That way I'm able to highlight areas that God speaks to me.

Many people make it a goal to go through the Bible in a year. I'll be honest: I've done it only a few times in my life. One reason this might be a challenge for people is that when we use a program to read the Bible daily and then we miss a few days, we try to make up for the times we missed by cramming more into the next time we open the Scriptures. If the gaps widen, we can feel overwhelmed by the sessions we do keep.

Do you know what that's like? Imagine missing six or seven meals. Then picture trying to make up for that in one sitting. On one plate you have some scrambled eggs and bacon. On another plate there is a steak, vegetables, and a salad. Then you have a bowl of pasta. You also have a chicken breast and fries . . .

There's no way you can stuff yourself with all these meals. And you won't be nourished the same way you would with a steady diet. The same goes for reading Scripture. You can't stuff yourself like that. You can't cram it all in just to hit a goal.

Instead, if you miss a day, tell yourself, *That's okay. I'll just read the Bible for today.* Don't try to make up for yesterday. Your goal is not to get through the Bible; your goal is to hear from God when you sit down to read. You want the Holy Spirit to reveal Jesus to you.

It's okay to spend thirty minutes on one verse. It's okay to spend several days without finishing a chapter.

The power of Scripture doesn't lie in the page count; the power resides when you listen closely to the passages and obey God's commands.

Get in the Word today and watch it transform your life.

Dear gracious, heavenly Father, thank You for speaking to me through Your Holy Word. You are the Author of Scripture, Lord. Forgive me for not listening closer to it and obeying Your commands. In Jesus' name, amen.

A Strong and Mighty Presence

"Oh, that they would always have hearts
like this, that they might fear me and obey
all my commands! If they did, they and their
descendants would prosper forever."

DEUTERONOMY 5:29 NLT

Have you ever experienced the way a room changes when a strong leader walks in? People tend to stand up straighter, watch what they say, listen with respect. The mere presence of a leader or someone in authority who can command a room inspires others to work harder, pay attention, and do their best.

When we spend time in God's presence every day, it changes how we think and act and obey.

Take Moses, for example. He experienced God's presence in an unfathomable, life-changing way.

After leading the children of Israel out of Egypt, Moses went up to Mount Sinai to meet with God (Exodus 19:3–10). Moses

When we spend time in God's presence every day, it changes how we think and act and obey.

spent precious time in the awesome presence of our Creator, and he heard God's desire to personally speak to His people and how to prepare for that meeting.

When God came down upon the mountain three days later, the people panicked and ran off. "Moses, we can't handle God," they told him. "We cannot be close to God, and we cannot hear the word from His mouth because we'll die. So you go talk to God. Tell us whatever He says."

Moses was heartbroken on behalf of the Israelites as he went back up to meet with God. But God said they were right, that they couldn't hear His voice or experience His presence, and He explained to Moses the reason behind their inability to enter His presence:

"Oh, that they would always have hearts like this, that they might fear me and obey all my commands! If they did, they and their descendants would prosper forever" (Deuteronomy 5:29 NLT).

God then commanded Moses to tell the Israelites to go back to their tents—to go back to playing church. But He also told Moses to stay close to Him so he could hear His voice. From that day forward, God's voice seemed like thunder to Israel, but to Moses, it was crystal clear (vv. 30–31). Over time Moses grew closer and closer to God while Israel grew more and more distant.

We may not have experienced God's glory in this dramatic way, but we can be in His presence every day. It's really the only way to know God the Father and His Son, Jesus. And by being in

His presence, we'll be transformed. Second Corinthians 3:18 says we are being transformed into His likeness from glory to glory. As we behold him, we become more like Him.

Spending time in God's presence changes everything.

Do you want to know how to become courageous as you head out into this crazy world today? Spend time in the Scriptures and see how awesome our God is, how He reveals Himself to His people. The more you can comprehend God's greatness, the greater your capacity will be to fear Him and live with bold faith.

Dear heavenly Father, thank You for Your presence in my life today. Help me to learn to dwell there and not just visit. May I see Your glory. I ask this in Jesus' name, amen.

PART 5

When You Need Courage to Fully Know and Revere God

DAY 41

Make an Impression

Charm is deceptive, and beauty does not last; but a woman who fears the Lord will be greatly praised.

PROVERBS 31:30 NLT

Advertisers love to point us to things of beauty and significance. Everywhere we go, we're bombarded with taglines and slogans promising unforgettable experiences and incredible offerings. Life, it seems, is about making favorable impressions and being remembered. The world tells us we should strive to have qualities people never forget.

The Bible makes it very clear what sort of qualities we should possess. If you look at the virtuous woman in Proverbs 31, she is full of many admirable traits, like being trustworthy and wise and hardworking and energetic. She exemplifies dignity in her presence. But what is her final virtue?

"Charm is deceptive, and beauty does not last; but a woman who fears the LORD will be greatly praised" (Proverbs 31:30 NLT).

The truth is, the significance that this woman has can be obtained by any man or woman who fears God.

There have been many leaders and popular personalities whom I have met over the years. I've interacted with pastors, speakers, and teachers who have impacted many lives. But the individuals who have had the most impact on me are those who have exemplified the true fear of God in their lives.

What does true beauty look like for you? What sort of things make a huge impression on you?

Holy fear and humility are the traits that bring honor and riches to your life. Wealth isn't measured in what we own but rather how we impact others. If you want to be remembered, embrace the character of Christ by continually pursuing the fear of the Lord.

Dear heavenly Father, thank You for all the beautiful things You have created in our world. Open my heart to see what true beauty is. Help me to be a person like the woman in Proverbs 31, clothed with dignity and the holy fear of You. In Jesus' name, amen.

DAY 42

The Most Valuable Treasure

The fear of the LORD is His treasure.

ISAIAH 33:6 NKJV

L et's do a hypothetical. What if fairy tales—in particular, the genie-in-the-bottle one—are true? You find a lamp, rub it, and out he comes! The genie enthusiastically proclaims, "Master, what do you wish for? Ask and it will be granted! Anything you request I will give to you!"

How would you answer? Many of us would ask for our family to be happy, healthy, and secure. We might ask for that dream vacation we've always wanted to take or a house in Beverly Hills. Some of us may think loftier and ask for positions of rulership, power, or great wealth.

Of course, that's all a myth, so let's return to reality. When Solomon was asked by God Almighty that very question, he didn't request happiness or wealth or a long life (1 Kings 3:5–12). Instead, Solomon asked for wisdom. He wrote, "Getting wisdom is the most important thing you can do" (Proverbs 4:7 GNT).

What led him to believe that? Let's probe deeper. Solomon's father, King David, taught him that the beginning of wisdom is the fear of the Lord (Psalm 111:10). This young ruler learned that holy fear was not only the starting place for but also the constant source of the instruction of wisdom (Proverbs 15:33). In asking for wisdom, Solomon was, in essence, asking for holy fear, and in doing so it propelled him to a level of success, fortune, and fame that was unmatched.

Solomon, one of the wisest and wealthiest men to have ever lived, was not only taught but also learned experientially that holy fear is the most valuable treasure we can possess (Ecclesiastes 12:13–14).

This treasure of holy fear and its wisdom has numerous benefits. It promotes longevity[1] and secures an eternal legacy.[2] It swallows up all other destructive fears, including the most dangerous: the fear of man.[3] It gives us confidence in difficult situations and a fearlessness that can face any adversity.[4] It keeps us safe and secure[5] as it provides angelic assistance.[6] It makes us productive and empowers us to multiply.[7] It fulfills our desires[8] and gives enduring success,[9] nobility,[10] and great influence. It promotes enjoyment of life and our labor,[11] true happiness,[12] and grants healing for our bodies.[13]*

Every one of these promises are made to those who walk in holy fear. No wonder it is called God's treasure!

Holy fear is not only the starting place for but also the constant source of wisdom.

Father God, give me holy fear that I may walk in Your wisdom and understanding. Help me know the truth of Isaiah 33:6, that "the fear of the LORD is [Your] treasure." Give me the wisdom and knowledge needed to live a life that is pleasing in Your sight. In Jesus' name, amen.

*Note: The scriptures making all of these promises are: 1) Proverbs 10:11; 2) Psalm 112:2–3; 3) Psalm 112:8; 4) Psalm 112:7–8; 5) Psalm 112:6; 6) Psalm 34:7; 7) Psalm 128:2; Psalm 25:12–13; 8) Psalm 145:19; 9) Psalm 112:3; 10) Proverbs 22:4; 11) Psalm 128:2; 12) Psalm 112:1; and 13) Proverbs 3:7–8.

DAY 43

Pursue Holiness

Therefore, having these promises,
beloved, let us cleanse ourselves from
all filthiness of the flesh and spirit,
perfecting holiness in the fear of God.

2 CORINTHIANS 7:1

The road to a courageous life is a narrow one. It involves pursuing holiness, and each side is lined with dangerous ditches, pitfalls we could easily fall into—legalism on one side and lawlessness on the other.

I observed the first pitfall years ago when the church at large was entrenched in legalism, promoting lifestyle requirements that were not scriptural and preaching a false gospel of salvation by works. A major revelation delivered us from this horrible trench: God is a good God.

But then the church did what humans often do—we went to the extreme opposite in our attempt to get as far from that legalistic trench as possible, and in doing so, we fell headlong into the lawlessness ditch. There we believed we were saved by an unscriptural grace that permits us to live no differently than the world. But this lie prevents us from experiencing the presence, blessing, and power of God.

For many, the word *holiness* carries a bad taste. It's either viewed as legalistic bondage or a virtue that's noble but unattainable. Some people think holiness is no fun and puts a damper on life, that pursuing it is a poor use of time. Sadly, these men and women don't see the beauty and strength of it. If they did, they would be chasing it.

It's easy to obey God in a church or a conference setting where His presence is strong. But what about those times when it's too easy to give in to sin? When temptation comes your way or anger strikes? When you're hurt by someone you love or when an opportunity to cheat suddenly arrives?

Pursing holiness begins in our hearts. It originates with our thoughts and motives and intentions, which all drive how we behave. This inner transformation is the only way we can ultimately begin to see God—to enter His glorious presence. If you tremble at God's Word and you walk in holy fear, you can live a holy life. For "by the fear of the LORD one departs from evil" (Proverbs 16:6).

A healthy Christian life is one that is based on the love of God and our fear of God. When we operate in these two virtues, we come into an intimate relationship with Him.

Holiness is true liberty, opening the way to enjoy God in this life.

Dear heavenly Father, forgive me for neglecting the pursuit of holiness. Help me to understand and to believe that chasing after holiness opens the door to an audience with You. Give me a reverent fear of You so that I can live the abundant life You've called me into. In Jesus' name, amen.

Equip Yourself Daily

Establish Your word to Your servant,
who is devoted to fearing You.

PSALM 119:38

What's the first thing you do when you wake up? Do you pick up your phone to check emails and messages? Do you scan through social media? Scroll through the news? Most of us probably spend more time on social media and online than we do in the Scriptures. We invest more time reading blogs and articles than we do reading God's Word.

I encourage you to do a little experiment. Consider what your day would look like if you started with Scripture instead of checking your phone first.

Our lives dramatically change when we spend time in God's Word. The more we can perceive and comprehend God's greatness, the more equipped we will be to face what the world throws at us. But in order to gain this knowledge, we must read the Bible. When we approach God's Word expectantly and prepared to find Him, we will encounter Him in an entirely new way. We're reminded in Jeremiah 29:13, "You will seek Me and find Me, when you search for Me with all your heart."

Unfortunately, many of us are not reading the Bible. The research company Barna, which regularly polls faith-based segments of the population, conducted a study in 2018 that revealed that only 48 percent of the people polled were Bible readers. Less than half of those surveyed read, listened to, or engaged with biblical content outside of a church service. Breaking down the stats even further, Barna Group found that 8 percent read the Bible three to four times a year, 6 percent once a month, 8 percent once a week, 13 percent several times a week, and 14 percent daily.[1]

I consider those who consistently and regularly read Scripture (daily or several times a week) to be healthy. Based on this research, that means only one-fourth of Christians in the US are really engaging with the Bible as they should.

Why do I only consider them to be healthy? Why not the people who read the Bible once a week or maybe once a month?

Could you survive by eating only one meal a week? You wouldn't be able to function properly. You wouldn't think clearly. If you ever had to fight to protect your family, you wouldn't have the strength. So just as physical food to our body is nourishment, the Word of God is nourishment to our spirit, which gives us a greater capacity to hear God.

Reading God's Word shouldn't just be something to check off a religious to-do list. We need to read God's Word because in it and through it we encounter Jesus, who is Himself the Word of Truth and the very source of our life. Make it your ambition and practice to get to know God through His Word, and you'll find yourself prepared for everything life throws at you.

Dear Lord, help me open the Bible so that I can seek You with my whole heart. Help me to approach Your Word expectantly and ready to find You. Equip me every day In Jesus' name, amen.

DAY 45

Behold God's Greatness

No one can measure his greatness.

PSALM 145:3 NLT

Consider the sunrise. Can you imagine trying to paint the sky every single morning with that palette of colors and those patterns of clouds? Not only every morning, but every moment of the day is a chance to behold the greatness of God. All of creation declares His glory.

Our holy fear grows proportionally to our comprehension of God's greatness.

God's glory is beyond understanding. It's unsearchable, has no boundaries or limitations, and is incomparable. Even so, when we seek to increase our comprehension of His greatness, we grow in holy fear, and subsequently, in courage. Scripture is full of examples of people proclaiming God's greatness:

The prophet Isaiah, when being transported to heaven and seeing the Lord seated on His throne, heard the angels shout out, "Holy, holy, holy is the LORD of Heaven's Armies! The whole earth is filled with his glory!" (Isaiah 6:3 NLT). They were so loud

Our holy fear grows proportionally to our comprehension of God's greatness.

in their cries, they shook the arena in heaven that seats over a billion beings.

Ezekiel saw the Lord and wrote, "This is what the glory of the LORD looked like to me. When I saw it, I fell face down on the ground" (Ezekiel 1:28 NLT).

When Abraham saw God, he "fell face down on the ground" (Genesis 17:3 NLT). And after God gloriously manifested on Sinai, "Moses himself was so frightened at the sight that he said, 'I am terrified and trembling'" (Hebrews 12:21 NLT).

John the apostle, the one Jesus loved, wrote of his encounter with our glorified Jesus, "When I saw him, I fell at his feet as if I were dead" (Revelation 1:17 NLT).

How do you view God's greatness? What posture do you assume? Do you stand in awe, or do you take Him for granted?

It's easy to be preoccupied with the onslaught of information of man's greatness that continually fills our minds. Our holy fear has been hindered by the world's system of desire, gain, and the pride of human achievements. We are continually bombarded by the glitz and glamour of talented athletes, beautiful Hollywood stars, gifted musicians, business gurus, charismatic leaders, and other important individuals.

All of these things deter us from the magnificent invitation to draw near and behold God.

Take time today to pause and gaze at His magnificence. When you do this, you'll find yourself enriched, strengthened, and at peace.

Dear heavenly Father, I ask that You reveal to me a fresh vision of Jesus. Help me to be conformed to the One who created the universe that I may behold Your greatness. May my holy fear increase as Your glory becomes more real. I ask this in Jesus' name, amen.

DAY 46

Live Out Your Song

Happy are those who hear the joyful call to worship, for they will walk in the light of your presence, Lᴏʀᴅ.

PSALM 89:15 ɴʟᴛ

W hat do you think of when you hear the word *worship*? Do you think of songs sung at church? Do you think of praise being the fast song and worship being the slow ones? Does the worship team on Sunday morning come to mind?

Worship isn't a song—it's obedience.

The first time worship is mentioned in the Bible is when Abraham told his servants that he and Isaac were going to the mountain to worship. But if you're familiar with the story, you know he wasn't going up there with his son to sing slow songs! He was obeying God's directive to sacrifice Isaac.

More than our hymns, God wants our hearts. God doesn't want our contemporary cool songs; He wants our submitted spirits.

Over the years, I've been in churches with amazing worship services—hundreds or thousands of believers gathered, with excellent praise and worship teams and skilled musicians and singers. But even if the services are innovative and high tech, the event creative and entertaining, the most significant element is missing if God's presence is nowhere to be found.

True worship is revealed by who we *obey*, not who we sing to. And if our lives on Monday don't reflect what we sang on Sunday, there is something drastically wrong.

A life of obedience is worship, and out of that life will flow songs that delight the heart of God. Worshiping God in truth comes not from our mouths but rather from our hearts. Worship is to fear and revere Him in the truest sense.

Remember today what the psalmist said: "Happy are those who hear the joyful call to worship, for they will walk in the light of your presence, Lord" (Psalm 89:15 NLT).

Dear heavenly Father, forgive me when my worship only comes on a Sunday. Help me to lead a life of worship. Help me to be consistently obedient to You so I can know You intimately as You manifest Yourself to me. Reveal Yourself to me. In Jesus' name, amen.

Joy and Gladness

My beloved . . . work out your own salvation with fear and trembling; for it is God who works in you both to will and to do for His good pleasure. Do all things without complaining.

PHILIPPIANS 2:12–14

Did you hear about the great pastor who once had a church of three million people yet only *two* adults in his congregation fulfilled their destiny? Sounds like a setup for a joke, but it's exactly what happened to Moses and the children of Israel—only Joshua and Caleb were allowed entrance into the promised land (Numbers 13). One of the reasons for this was because the Israelites complained.

Perhaps you've never paid attention to the five sins that kept Israel from their destiny: craving evil things, worshiping idols, sexual immorality, testing God, and complaining (1 Corinthians 10:6–10).

If you're like me, you might think, *What? Complaining? How can complaining be included in a list with these other massive sins?*

But the Holy Spirit convicted me: *John, complaining is a serious sin in My eyes.* He showed me that when I complain, I'm basically saying, "God, I don't like what You are doing in my life, and if I were You I would do things differently."

It is an affront to My character, the Holy Spirit told me. *It's rebellion to My will, and it's a gross lack of holy fear.*

The children of Israel complained constantly. They were displeased with the way they were being led and what was transpiring in their lives. They blamed God for their discomfort, lack, and anything else that wasn't gratifying. They lacked holy fear; they didn't tremble at His Word.

God said to them: "Because you did not serve the LORD your God with joy and gladness of heart, for the abundance of everything, therefore you shall serve your enemies" (Deuteronomy 28:47–48).

The only one who can get you out of the will of God—out of fulfilling your destiny—is you. No man or woman, no child, no demon, no institution . . . just you. Joseph's brothers tried to destroy his dream, but the call of God stayed intact because Joseph feared and believed God. Even though Joseph suffered hardship, we never see any evidence of one complaint from him.

Complaining is a killer. It will short-circuit the life God has for you faster than almost any other thing! Complaining is the antithesis of holy fear. We dishonor God and His Word when we think or speak from the posture of discontent.

Trembling at God's Word involves joy and gladness at the core of our being. If absent, it's only a matter of time before circumstances reveal the lack of joy and gratitude.

Dear gracious, heavenly Father, forgive me for the times I've complained or murmured or grumbled. Help me to be at peace and content with everything You're doing in my life. I make the choice to follow hard after You in order to fulfill the destiny You have for me. I choose to do this with an attitude of joy and gratefulness. In Jesus' name, amen.

Marvel at God's Presence

Therefore, since we are receiving a kingdom which cannot be shaken, let us have grace, by which we may serve God acceptably with reverence and godly fear. For our God is a consuming fire.

HEBREWS 12:28–29

It used to be very difficult for me to enter God's presence in my times of prayer. But one day I started doing something, practically by accident. I decided not to begin my time of prayer singing or uttering any words. I merely pondered the awesomeness and holiness of our God.

You measured the universe with the span of Your hand. From Your thumb to Your pinky, You weighed the mountains. You measured every drop of water on the planet in the palm of Your hands. You placed the stars in their orbits with Your fingers and called every one of them by name.

The way to enter into the presence of God is through reverence— holy, awesome reverence.

God, You are awesome!

Almost immediately I was met with His presence. I didn't see it coming, and it surprised me. I decided to do the same thing the next day and experienced the same result. And on the third day, it happened again.

I was baffled.

"Lord," I prayed, "why has it been so easy for me the past three days to come into Your presence?"

The Spirit of God reminded me of how Jesus taught His disciples to pray with the Lord's Prayer: "Our Father in heaven, hallowed be Your name . . ."

I yelled out, "That's it! Jesus taught His disciples to come into the presence of God with holy awe and reverence!"

It then made total sense to me. The way to enter into the presence of God is through reverence. Holy, awesome reverence.

Later this decree became more real to me: "'By those who come near Me I must be regarded as holy'" (Leviticus 10:3). I realize this is an eternal decree, one that has always been and one that will always be.

Do you revere God when you come to His presence, whether in prayer, a small group, or church?

Do you honor God by the way you live?

Are the things that are important to God important to you?

Do you embrace His heart and love what He loves?

Do you disdain what God disdains?

Do you ponder Who He really is—the One you call "Father"?

Dear glorious and majestic Father, hallowed is Your name. You are awesome! You are wonderful! You are holy! Forgive me for the times I've taken Your presence for granted. I want to be aware of and respect Your presence no matter where I am or what I'm doing. I want to live in reverent awe of You at all times. I ask this in Jesus' name, amen.

Pursue God's Friendship

Come close to God, and God will come close to you.

JAMES 4:8 NLT

When was the last time you spoke to your best friend or sent them a message? If you're like me, your best friend is someone with whom you share important details and your most intimate secrets. You're in regular communication with them and you share things you wouldn't share with anyone else.

God wants an intimate relationship with you. Psalm 25:14 says, "The *secret* of the LORD is with those who fear Him, and He will show them His covenant" (emphasis added).

The Hebrew word for "secret" is *sôd* and is defined as "counsel." God's secret counsel—the sharing of His secrets—is with His close, intimate friends. But God is not everyone's friend, only those who fear Him.

It's easy for people to talk about God as if He's a buddy to hang out with. There are people I know who can fill me in on the facts and details of a celebrity's life, but that doesn't mean they're friends with them. It's the same with God. We can attend church services and lead youth group and read our Bibles daily, but that doesn't guarantee friendship with God.

God isn't looking for likes on His social media account or for buddies. He's looking for an intimate relationship with those who fear him.

As we've shared in this book, two men in the Old Testament are identified as God's friends: Abraham and Moses. Their lives exemplify the path that leads to friendship with the Lord. They demonstrate the parameters placed on a friendship with Jesus, who didn't say, "You are all My friends if you believe I am the Christ." Rather, Jesus said, "You are My friends if you do whatever I command you" (John 15:14). Both Abraham and Moses, out of holy fear, obeyed what God commanded them to do and they experienced an intimate friendship with God.

God deeply desires to be close with each of us, but true intimacy requires both parties knowing each other well, not just one. Just as God searches our innermost thoughts, we should also strive for true familiarity with our heavenly Father.

Look at what Moses said about this level of relationship: "You have told me, 'I know you by name, and I look favorably on you.' If it is true that you look favorably on me, let me know your ways so I may understand you more fully and continue to enjoy your favor" (Exodus 33:12–13 NLT). Moses longed for a deep and intimate relationship with God.

Pursue God's friendship, but do so in a way that keeps awe and reverence for Him at the forefront. Don't become so casual with the Holy God or bring Him down to our level by calling Him your Savior and your buddy all in the same breath.

Dear heavenly Father, today I choose to pursue knowing You the way You have chosen to know me. Help me know You through Your Word and in spending time with You in prayer today. I ask this In Jesus' name, amen.

DAY 50

Finish Well

Listen to me and do as I say, and you
will have a long, good life.

PROVERBS 4:10 NLT

"Finishing is better than starting."

Solomon wrote these words in Ecclesiastes 7:8 (NLT). Picture the king at the end of his life reflecting. I think we can all agree that when looking back it is easier to identify pitfalls than it is looking forward before meeting them. The Lord appeared to Solomon twice and told him to ask for anything he wanted. Solomon prayed to have an understanding heart so he could distinguish good from evil. Yet we later learn that he chose not to endure and ended up becoming a cynic. He essentially said, "Nothing changes . . . Everything's boring, utterly boring . . . There's nothing new—it's the same old story . . . Don't count on being remembered."

Solomon was the wisest man who ever lived, other than Jesus. He knew that "the fear of the LORD is the beginning of knowledge," as he wrote in Proverbs 1:7. He would go on to achieve heights no human being before or since has even come close to accomplishing. Despite all this, he faltered in the latter part of his reign and his life. And when he finally looked back in lament, he emphasized the fear of God at the end of Ecclesiastes:

"Here now is my final conclusion: Fear God and obey his commands, for this is everyone's duty" (Ecclesiastes 12:13 NLT).

It's clear that the fear of God is all about finishing well. This is why we are told, "The fear of the LORD is clean, enduring forever" (Psalm 19:9). In the Christian life, the ultimate finish is to hear our Lord say to us, "Well done, My good and faithful servant!"

Always remember, it's not how we start this race that's most important, but how we finish it. Scripture is full of heartbreaking examples of those who started well but didn't finish well.

But we can take great hope in this: "Now all glory to God, who is *able* to keep you from falling away and will bring you with great joy into his glorious presence without a single fault" (Jude v. 24 NLT, emphasis added)

Finishing well is the most important aspect of living well. Notice Jude said that God is *able*—in other words, our cooperation is essential. God, through His gift of holy fear, is *able* to keep us strong and blameless to the end. God wants to protect us from the traps of life. He wants us to faithfully endure, yet we must cooperate with His grace to see this result.

I love the word *endurance*. We hear this theme shouted in the New Testament. Jesus said, "But the one who endures to the end will be saved" (Matthew 24:13 NLT). We see the apostle Paul in almost every letter talking about enduring. "But you must continue to believe this truth and stand firmly in it. Don't drift away from the assurance you received when you heard the Good News" (Colossians 1:23 NLT).

Christianity is not a sprint; it's an endurance run. Hebrews 12 tells us to shed every weight that slows us down, especially our sins. We are told to "run with *endurance* the race God has set before us" (v. 1 NLT, emphasis added). I love verses 2 and 3 from *The Message:*

> Never quit! . . . Keep your eyes on Jesus, who both began and finished this race we're in. Study how he did it. Because he never lost sight of where he was headed—that exhilarating finish in and with God—he could put up with anything along the way. . . . When you find yourselves flagging in your faith, go over that story again, item by item, that long litany of hostility he plowed through. That will shoot adrenaline into your souls!

Never lose sight of where you are headed. Remember that the key to finishing strong is endurance. Continue to remain steadfast, no matter the difficulty, hardship, or length of time.

Never lose
sight of
where you
are headed.
Remember
that the key to
finishing strong
is endurance
and remaining
steadfast.

Dear heavenly Father, please give me the strength and resolve to endure to the end. Fill me with the spirit of the fear of the Lord that I may finish well and bring You glory. In Jesus' name, amen.

Notes

Day 3: Following Christ at All Costs
1. Peter M. Peterson, *Andrew, Brother of Simon Peter: His History and Legends* (Leiden: Brill, 1958)
2. John Foxe, *Foxe's Christian Martyrs of the World* (Greensburg, PA. Barbour and Company, 1991), 6–7.

Day 4: Courage When It Counts
1. Herbert Musurillo, trans., *The Acts of the Christian Martyrs* (Oxford University Press, 1972).

Day 7: Chase Away All Other Fears
1. Charles H. Spurgeon, *The Complete Works of C. H. Spurgeon, Volume 13: Sermons 728 to 787* (Delmarva Publications, 2015), 308.

Day 8: Follow His Command
1. Hudson Taylor, *A Retrospect*, 3rd ed. (Toronto: China Inland Mission, n.d.), 119–20.
2. N. Gist Gee, *The Educational Directory for China* (Suzhou: Educational Association of China, 1905), 43.
3. Paul Borthwick, *Leading the Way* (Colorado Springs, CO: Navpress, 1989), 153.

Day 9: Pursue God's Word
1. Tim Chaffey, "3. Unity of the Bible," *Answers Magazine*, April 1, 2011, https://answersingenesis.org/the-word-of-god/3-unity-of-the-bible/.

Notes

Day 12: Proclaim the Truth

1. "Biblical Commentaries: Matthew 14," StudyLight.org, https://www.studylight.org/commentaries/eng/rwp/matthew-14.html.

Day 15: The Strength to Resist

1. "Biography," International Bonhoeffer Society, accessed June 14, 2023, https://bonhoeffersociety.org/about/bonhoeffer/biography/.
2. Dietrich Bonhoeffer, "After Ten Years" in *Letters & Papers From Prison* (New York: Simon and Schuster, 1997), 11.
3. Eric Metaxas, *Bonhoeffer: Pastor, Martyr, Prophet, Spy* (Nashville, TN: Thomas Nelson, 2020), 532.

Day 17: Beware of Pride

1. A. W. Tozer, *I Call It Heresy: And Other Timely Topics from First Peter* (Camp Hill, PA: Wing Spread Publishers, 1991).

Day 19: Strength for Hard Times

1. Elizabeth Keckley, *Behind the Scenes: Or, Thirty Years a Slave and Four Years in the White House* (London: Partridge and Oakey, 1868).
2. Keckley, *Behind the Scenes.*
3. Abraham Lincoln, *Collected Works of Abraham Lincoln, Volume 7.*

Day 20: Overcome Defeat

1. Foxe, John, 1516–1587. *Foxe's Book of Martyrs, or, The Acts and Monuments of the Christian Church: Being a Complete History of the Lives, Sufferings, and Deaths of the Christian Martyrs . . . to Which Is Added an Account of the Inquisition . . . with the Lives of Some of the Early Eminent Reformers* (Philadelphia: J.B. Smith, 1856).

2. Works of William Tyndale, vol. 1, p. 135.

3. Foxe, page 152.

Day 25: Pray Courageously

1. Saint Augustine of Hippo, *The Confessions of Saint Augustine, Book III* (Mount Vernon, NY: Peter Pauper Press), chapter 11.

Day 32: Don't Give Up

1. "William Wilberforce's 1789 Abolition Speech," Brycchancarey. com, accessed June 13, 2023, https://www.brycchancarey.com /abolition/wilberforce2.htm.

2. William Wilberforce, *Real Christianity: Discerning True Faith from False Beliefs* (Minneapolis, MN: Bethany House, 1987).

3. Wilberforce, *Real Christianity.*

Day 34: Swim Against the Tide

1. "Crusade City Spotlight: Chicago," Billy Graham Library, February 6, 2013, https://billygrahamlibrary.org/crusade-city -spotlight-chicago/.

Day 35: Walk Through the Fire

1. Henry Arnaud and Jaques Brez, *Authentic details of the Valdenses, in Piemont and other countries; with abridged translations of "L'histoire des Vaudois," par Bresse, and La rentree glorieuse, d'Henri Arnaud, with the ancient Valdensian catechism, to which are subjoined original letters, written during a residence among the Vaudois of Piemont and Wirtemberg, in 1825* (London: J. Hatchard and Son, 1827).

2. James D. McCabe Jr., *Cross and Crown: Sufferings and Triumphs of the Heroic Men and Women who Were Persecuted for the Religion of Jesus Christ* (Cincinnati, OH: National Publishing Company, 1873).

Notes

Day 39: Spend Time in the Word

1. Dwight L. Moody, *Pleasure and Profit in Bible Study* (Chicago: Moody, 2013), 8.
2. Arnold Cole and Pamela Caudill Ovwigho, "Understanding the Bible Engagement Challenge: Scientific Evidence for the Power of 4," Center for Biblical Engagement, December 2009, https://bttbfiles.com/web/docs/cbe/Scientific_Evidence_for_the_Power_of_4.pdf.

Day 44: Equip Yourself Daily

1. "State of the Bible 2018: Seven Top Findings," Barna Group, July 10, 2018, https://www.barna.com/research/state-of-the-bible-2018-seven-top-findings/.

Acknowledgments

I'm grateful to HarperCollins Christian Publishing for their partnership in publishing this work. I appreciate the hard work of the Gift team, and especially Jennifer Gott, Kara Mannix, Sabryna Lugge, Kristen Parrish, Emily Ghattas, Kristi Smith, Lydia Eagle, and MacKenzie Collier.

A special thanks to Travis Thrasher for helping me compile each day's devotion. You are an amazing writer and researcher.

Thank you to my agent, Esther Fedorkevich, for believing in this message and encouraging me to write it.

Lastly, thank you to Lisa and my family and the Messenger team, who have consistently supported me. I love each of you dearly.

About the Author

Photo courtesy of Messenger International

John Bevere is a minister known for his bold, uncompromising approach to God's Word. He is also an international bestselling author who has written more than 20 books that have collectively sold millions of copies and been translated into over 130 languages.

Along with his wife, Lisa, John is the co-founder of Messenger International, a ministry committed to revolutionizing global discipleship. Driven by a passion to develop uncompromising followers of Christ, Messenger has given over 60 million translated resources to leaders across the globe. To extend these efforts, the MessengerX app was developed, providing digital discipleship resources at no cost to users in more than 120 languages. MessengerX currently has users in over 20,000 cities and over 235 nations.

When John is home in Franklin, Tennessee, you'll find him loving on his g-babies, playing pickleball, or trying to persuade Lisa to take up golf.

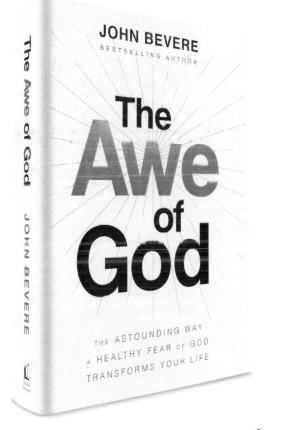

Free Courses, Audiobooks, and More to Help You Grow in Your Faith.

The MessengerX app is a revolutionary tool that connects you with world-class teachers, authors, and leaders who will help you embrace a vibrant faith in your everyday life.

Scan the QR code to dowload MessengerX

MessengerX

11:59

drawing near
A life of intimacy with God

JOHN BEVERE

Drawing Near

John Bevere

God desires a close relationship with us! But far too many settle for a shallow one when God has extended an invitation to draw near, so we can all experience greater depths of intimacy with Him. Learn how you can transform a boring and lifeless relationship with that is energizing and exhilarating!